Democracy at Work

Democracy at Work:

A Cure for Capitalism

Richard Wolff

Haymarket Books
Chicago, Illinois

Democracy at Work: A Cure for Capitalism
© 2012 Richard Wolff

Haymarket Books
P.O. Box 180165
Chicago, IL 60618
773-583-7884
info@haymarketbooks.org
www.haymarketbooks.org

ISBN:978-1-60846-247-6

Trade distribution:
In the U.S. through Consortium Book Sales and Distribution, www.cbsd.com
In Canada, Publishers Group Canada, www.pgcbooks.ca
In the UK, Turnaround Publisher Services, www.turnaround-psl.com
In Australia, Palgrave Macmillan, www.palgravemacmillan.com.au
All other countries, Publishers Group Worldwide, www.pgw.com

This book was published with the generous support of
the Wallace Global Fund and the Lannan Foundation.

Printed in Canada by union labor.

Library of Congress CIP Data is available.

10 9 8 7 6 5 4 3

RECYCLED
Paper made from
recycled material
FSC
www.fsc.org   FSC® C103567

Contents

Introduction

Cascading economic problems and crises, coupled with dysfunctional political responses, have plunged modern societies into deepening turmoil. Capitalism—the dominant economic system of our time—has once again become the subject of criticism and opposition. A global capitalist system that no longer meets most people's needs has prompted social movements everywhere to arise and coalesce in the active search for systemic alternatives. Yet the particular versions of anticapitalism—the various forms of state socialism and communism—that actually prevailed over the last century no longer seem to offer a model or inspiration to those looking for an alternative to capitalism. People are looking for a new solution, a new cure for capitalism's injustices, waste, and massive breakdowns. This book offers one such cure.

In presenting the idea of workers' self-directed enterprises (which I will call WSDEs throughout this book), I offer a new version of an old idea: that production works best when performed by a community that collectively and democratically designs and carries out shared labor. In analyzing capitalism to show its shortcomings and in establishing how WSDEs would overcome them, I use Karl Marx's theory of the production, appropriation, and distribution of the surplus, his "class analysis."* This is also a book with a political purpose: I seek to add the expansion of WSDEs to contemporary programs for progressive social change. I do not offer examinations of the countless past and present examples of collective or cooperative enterprises or of their contemporary counterparts. A rich literature on such projects is available in many reference documents.† In contrast, this book about workers' self-directed enterprise analyzes WSDEs in relation to capitalism and advocates them as a superior way to organize production.

The United States has recently suffered five years of the worst economic crisis since the Great Depression of the 1930s. For most people, the end of this crisis is not in sight. Tens of millions remain unemployed, many for extended lengths of time. Unprecedented numbers of foreclosed and homeless people live not far from unprecedented numbers of homes that stand empty. Wages and benefits

---

* "Surplus" is the excess of the value added by workers' labor—and taken by the employer—over the value paid in wages to them. To pay a worker $10 per hour, an employer must receive more than $10 worth of extra output per hour to sell. Surplus is capitalists' revenue net of direct input and labor costs to produce output; enterprise profits represent one portion of the surplus. For fuller expositions, see Stephen Resnick and Richard Wolff, *Knowledge and Class: A Marxian Critique of Political Economy* (New York and London: Routledge, 1987), chapter 3, and the same authors' *Contending Economic Theories: Neoclassical, Keynesian, and Marxian* (Cambridge: MIT University Press, 2012).

† See Immanuel Ness and Dario Azzellini, eds., *Ours to Master and to Own: Workers' Control from the Commune to the Present* (Chicago: Haymarket Books, 2011), and also www.democracyatwork.info.

are trending downward while profits are simultaneously increasing. Just as these conditions force millions to need and want more from local, state, and federal governments, officials continue to announce ever more cutbacks in public services. This crisis is reminding millions about capitalism's inherent instability, its historic failure for centuries to prevent the recurrence of downturns, and how poorly, unjustly, and cruelly it typically "manages" them.

A Tale of Two Crises

The current economic crisis comes after a period of thirty years during which business interests rolled back the New Deal that saved capitalism during the Great Depression of the 1930s. There is more than a little irony in that story. The three years after the 1929 crash both shook and ended capitalism's roaring 1920s, as well as the Republicans' hold on the presidency. A centrist Democrat, Franklin D. Roosevelt, became president. He and his party worried—as did Republicans then—about deficits and balancing Washington budgets. FDR began his presidency acting much like most leading Democrats today. But the Depression provoked and strengthened forces that changed him. Those forces both pressed him and enabled him to change his policies and thereby become the most progressive and the most popular president in US history.

The Great Depression provoked the formation and immense successes of the Congress of Industrial Organizations (CIO). The CIO organized millions of industrial workers into unions for the first time, bringing about the greatest unionization wave in US history. Members and leaders agreed that unions were working people's best weapons against the ravages of a severely depressed capitalism. They confronted employers (with job actions, strikes, and collective bargaining) and politicians (by mobilizing union members and their money for both electoral and non-electoral campaigns). The CIO's demands for jobs and for direct government help to the average American changed political conditions in the 1930s. The CIO undermined the conservative or centrist Democratic program of the time (what today would be called "austerity").

The Great Depression also drove into high gear a variety of socialist and communist groups, movements, and parties. Inside and outside the CIO, they mobilized large numbers of workers, students, farmers, and others. These left organizations mixed (1) public campaigns for jobs and better living conditions for the mass of Americans, (2) systematic electoral work, often coordinated with the CIO and other unions, and (3) more or less revolutionary demands aimed at transition from capitalism to socialism.

Together, the CIO, socialists, and communists made it impossible to continue policies that "managed" the Great Depression by bailing out the banks and major corporations, keeping government economic intervention otherwise minimal, and leaving the unemployed and foreclosed basically unassisted. At the same time, the CIO, socialists, and communists brought millions into the streets shaking their fists. They criticized business and capitalism more and more intensely. Those actions prompted and enabled FDR to present big business and the richest citizens (the business and power elite that included his own family) with a plan.

On the one hand, they could accommodate FDR's demands for taxes on business and the rich to be used to meet major social welfare demands of the CIO, socialists, and communists. FDR believed he could thereby satisfy enough mass social needs to preserve the capitalist ownership and production systems intact, though they would be more regulated than before. On the other hand, if big business and the rich refused, FDR warned that they would soon face a population led by increasingly anticapitalist forces seeking much more fundamental changes to the system.

FDR's plan split the ranks of big business and the rich. Enough of them agreed to higher taxes on business and the rich to allow FDR to offer a parallel deal to the left. He urged them to be reformers, not revolutionaries: to keep demands for going beyond capitalism at the level of rhetoric but not take them into practical politics.

FDR built a powerful political partnership between that part of big business and the rich he had won over and the unions and the left, despite some dissenters on both sides of the equation. That partnership never fundamentally challenged boards of directors' dominant control over US corporations. Major private shareholders continued to select boards of directors who continued to make the basic decisions of what, how, and where to produce and where to distribute the surpluses they appropriated from their workers.

FDR's partnership proceeded to construct a kind of social democracy or welfare state in the United States, a genuine New Deal. FDR promised that such a program would get US capitalism out of the Depression, provide better lives to most Americans quickly, and prevent future depressions. The only alternative to the New Deal, FDR warned, would be deepening economic and social divisions, tensions, and conflicts.

The partnership was crafted from both sides. One side was comprised of business leaders and wealthy citizens, led by FDR, who believed it necessary and expedient to accommodate left forces unleashed and strengthened by the Depression. On the other side were those leaders of the CIO, socialist, and communist movements who saw reform as the most that could be accomplished and revolution as premature at best and far too dangerous a gamble at worst. To

FDR's right, a considerable number of big businesses and rich Americans rejected his political partnership and steadfastly opposed its social democratic program. To FDR's left, some radicals and revolutionaries also rejected the partnership as a reformist sellout of the movement to overturn capitalism.

FDR's partnership prevailed politically. In the depths of the Great Depression, it launched costly programs that helped many millions (especially remarkable given what has not happened in the economic crisis since 2007). An expensive Social Security system was established to provide public pensions to the mass of US workers. An expensive federal unemployment insurance system was established to directly assist the unemployed. Expensive federal hiring programs were established that created and filled more than twelve million jobs during the Depression years after 1934. At a time when employers, employees, and government officials all complained of depleted revenues and funds, Washington found and spent vast sums directly to ease the suffering of working people and to stimulate a deeply depressed economy.

It was not a shortage of money that had previously prevented the government from helping people. The problem was, rather, political, and FDR's partnership provided a solution. It saved US capitalism from the risks of insufficient private-sector demand and of major social conflict between the devotees of capitalism and an angry working class that was better organized and mobilized than ever before or since. When the opposition of business and the rich limited what FDR's partnership could achieve after 1937, the United States' entry into World War II again split and weakened that opposition.

In the current crisis of capitalism, an FDR-type solution has not emerged, for several reasons. First, the fifty-year decline and consequent weakness of the labor union movement and the extreme decline of socialist and communist movements removed them as effective agents for such a solution. During his first term in office, President Obama did not even propose, let alone implement, any federal hiring programs, and supported the contraction, not expansion, of Social Security benefits. Second, the majority of businesses and the rich see little need—yet—for any compromise solution that would increase their taxes. Third, no actually existing socialism (such as the Soviet Union represented during the 1930s) poses an alternative today that might attract significant working-class support and thereby frighten conservatives into FDR-type political partnerships.

Political Dysfunction Worsens Economic Dysfunction

The absence of a left-wing force from below has left the United States with a severe crisis but without government intervention adequate to sustain a broad economic recovery. Instead, continued mainstream faith in neoliberal and neoclassical economics, which oppose government intervention on principle, yields insufficient fiscal stimulus measures coupled with overreliance on government debt. Meanwhile, the Federal Reserve's monetary policy pumps massive sums into support for banks and global credit markets. This program seeks to save and bolster the largest businesses (both financial and nonfinancial), the stock markets, and the richest 5 percent of individuals who depend on those businesses and markets. These beneficiaries of public policy are also the key financiers for US political parties, candidates, and officials. The latter devise and execute this rather classic example of a "trickle-down economics" program. Large and direct government assistance for business and the rich is supposed to "trickle down" and provide a recovery for the mass of people, too.

However, the trickle-down economics program hasn't worked—and for reasons that are not hard to discern. The government-enhanced wealth at the top does not "trickle down" in the real world. Instead, boards of directors continue to see their self-interest in not sharing the recovery funds poured into their hands. Thus we experience continuing high unemployment, massive numbers of home foreclosures, declining real wages and job benefits, and inaccessibility of credit for personal borrowing. Stagnant consumption and investment are the results. They undermine the recovery of business and the stock markets. The global capitalist crisis deepens.

What is to be done? The political and economic establishment simply repeats its usual mainstream mantra: maintain the post-2007 trickle-down program with maximum hype about the government's efforts to end the crisis and wait until the crisis depresses wages and the costs of doing business enough that profit opportunities prompt capitalists to resume investing. The establishment prefers to wait rather than to pay the costs of a government intervention sufficient to overcome the crisis. Capitalism, it insists, will eventually produce an economic upturn.

An alternative, though predictable and inadequate, program has come from the still-small but growing coterie of Keynesians. They have been reinvigorated by this crisis much as John Maynard Keynes's intervention, their inspiration, was produced by the 1930s crisis. They want a much bigger government fiscal stimulus paid for by bigger temporary budget deficits. They insist that the rising national debt can easily be offset later, once robust economic growth resumes. They are quite confident that a bigger stimulus will solve what they see as the problem: returning to a "normal" capitalism from a crisis-ridden capitalism.

The struggle in Washington continues between a somewhat

crisis-weakened but still dominant mainstream and its very moderate Keynesian critics. Both sides speak and act as if their positions mark the limits of legitimate debate and fully exhaust the space of economic policy options. It took the explosion of Occupy Wall Street to open that space to the other—nonmainstream and non-Keynesian—options. These options were always available but have been long repressed by business interests and their political, media, and academic allies. This book is devoted to one of those other options.

As an enduring crisis brings economic suffering to most American families, the political system shows less and less capacity to solve the root problem. Indeed, growing numbers of Americans see the political debates in Washington as irrelevant or even detrimental to their concerns. The mainstream trickle-down policies of George W. Bush and Barack Obama appear to have pandered to corporations and the rich while bypassing recovery for the vast majority. Because massive government borrowing helped to pay for those policies, national deficits and debt rose quickly. Now both political parties bicker over the details of austerity to reduce those deficits and that debt. They debate larger versus smaller cutbacks in public services and public employment.

In short, Americans have suffered from years of an economic crisis they did not cause. They have watched a recovery program that did not help them. They have been lectured by the architects of that recovery program on the need for "everyone" to pay its costs. And then the mass of Americans learned that "everyone" means them—not the people whose actions caused the crisis—and that they must suffer austerity cutbacks just when they urgently need more and better government services. No wonder the prospect of alternative Keynesian policies running up still-larger deficits and debts and thereby risking worse austerity measures is unattractive to so many.

The Delusion of Regulation

Broadly defined, the government intervenes economically by regulating the economic interactions among and between enterprises and individuals. It does this by taxing their activities (earning income, owning wealth, spending money, and so on) and by making rules governing those activities. However, the real contents and effects of government regulations depend on the interests that govern their design and implementation.

The New Deal–era taxes on business and the rich and regulations of enterprise behavior proved vulnerable and unsustainable. The enemies of the New Deal had the incentives (profit maximization) and the resources (their returns on investments) to undo many of its reforms after World War II, with ever-greater effect in the period since the 1970s. They systematically evaded, then weakened, the taxes and regulations of the New Deal, and eventually, when politically possible, eliminated them altogether. Business profits funded the parties, politicians, public relations campaigns, and professional think tanks that together shaped the real social effects and historical decline of government economic regulation. Examples include the destruction of the Glass-Steagall Act, the current assault on Social Security, the shift in the federal tax burden from business to individuals and from upper- to middle-income individuals, and so on.

Unions, the left, and the progressive wing of the Democratic Party—even when in power—proved unable or unwilling to secure the federal government's commitment to New Deal policies. Proposals for "new" New Deals therefore strike many today as fundamentally inadequate given that the system's dominant institutions—capitalist corporations—retain the incentives and keep obtaining the resources to undo any such New Deals. To the dismay of Keynesians, their critiques of mainstream economic policies and proposals of new New

Deals draw little enthusiasm or support. Regulation, deregulation, and reregulation strike ever more Americans as a delusional misunderstanding of where the basic problem lies.

A Cure for Capitalism

An increasing number of people are seeking a very different solution to the economic and political morass engulfing the United States and beyond. For them, that solution must have several key components. One is a permanent end to the periodic crises generated by capitalism (promised repeatedly but never achieved by its leaders over the last century). Another component is an economic system reorganized to secure greater income and wealth equality. Still another component is a genuinely democratic distribution of power among individuals inside both their workplaces and their communities.

To achieve this solution requires, first, a comprehensive critique of how capitalism works to yield its unacceptable outcomes. Second, we need a vision of an alternative economic system free of capitalism's structural flaws. That system would constitute a cure for capitalism. It would overcome its otherwise intractable problems. This book uses and builds on Marx's critique of capitalism because, notwithstanding its limits, it remains the most developed and useful critique available. The cure I advocate here is also informed by several traditions: movements for social justice, traditions of working-class protest against capitalism, and movements for cooperative economic action (purchasing, owning, and producing).

This cure involves, first, replacing the current capitalist organization of production inside offices, factories, stores, and other workplaces in modern societies. In short, exploitation—the production of a surplus appropriated and distributed by those other than its producers—would stop. Much as earlier forms of class structure (lords exploiting serfs in feudalism and masters exploiting slaves in slavery) have been abolished, the capitalist class structure (employers exploiting wage laborers) would have to be abolished, as well.

In corporations, the dominant form of modern capitalist enterprises, no longer would small boards of directors selected by a typically tiny number of major shareholders appropriate and distribute the surplus produced by employees. Instead, the surplus-producing workers themselves would make the basic decisions about production and distribution. They would become, collectively and democratically, their own board of directors. Shareholder-selected boards would no longer direct what, how, and where the enterprise produces. Instead, all of the workers in enterprises—those directly producing outputs and those providing the support services enabling production—would collectively become the directors deciding what, where, and how to produce and how to distribute the appropriated surpluses. Capitalist enterprises would thereby be transformed into workers' self-directed enterprises (WSDEs).

Secondly, such reorganized production sites would partner with similarly democratic organizations of residential communities interdependent with WSDEs. Because the decisions reached in WSDEs would affect residents in these communities and vice versa, a genuine democracy would require each interacting partner to participate in decisions reached by the other. Codetermination by workplace and community democracies would become the new reality of social self-governance.

Among the major social decisions to be so codetermined would be the following: (1) what mix of private and socialized property in the means of production would be best, (2) what mix of markets and planning would be preferred as means of distributing resources and products, and (3) what mix of representative and direct democratic decision-making should exist within both workplaces and residential communities. The democracies at both social sites would make and continually adjust these decisions collaboratively.

Such a reorganization of workplaces, coupled with the institutionalization of democratic codetermination, would effectively end capitalism. It would mark yet another milestone in human history, following the earlier transitions out of slavery and feudalism as organizations of production. The disappearances of slaves and masters and lords and serfs would now be replicated by the disappearance of capitalists and workers. Such oppositional categories would no longer apply to the relationships of production. Instead, workers would become their own collective bosses. The two categories—employer and employee—would be integrated within the same individuals.

At the same time, reorganizing workplaces in this way would be different from the historic efforts in the twentieth century to go beyond capitalism. Unlike those traditional state forms of socialism and communism, it would no longer be enough to just nationalize productive property and replace markets with central planning. The crucial additional—and hence transformative—element would be the reorganization of all workplace enterprises to eliminate exploitation. Instituting WSDEs would structurally position workers as appropriators and distributors of any surpluses they generated.

The state would thus become dependent for its revenues, operation, and very existence on receiving distributions of portions of the surpluses from the self-directed workers themselves. The power imbalance between states and their populations that haunted the last century of socialism and communism would thereby be structurally overcome. In this way, we could establish the material basis for the eventual withering away of the state that many Marxists envisage.

Reorganizing production so that workers become collectively self-directed at their worksites moves society beyond both capitalism and the last century's actually existing socialisms and communisms. In that sense, WSDEs represent an alternative to both capitalism and traditional state socialism/communism, an alternative to systems that accord directing power inside enterprises either to private capitalists elected by shareholders or to state capitalists selected by government or party. In WSDEs, decisions about production and distribution of outputs no longer primarily serve small subgroups (receivers of profits, dividends, and capital gains) rather than the majority of workers and their communities. Social criteria—democratically determined by self-directed workers and community members—would replace the drive for profit and accumulation in investment and all other economic decisions.

All workers would now have two job descriptions. First, they would be democratically and collectively assigned a specific production task (usually for a specific time period) within the workplace division of labor. Second, they would be democratically and collectively given fully equal participation throughout their term of employment in the design, operation, and change of that division of labor and in the distribution of its outputs. No one could work without engaging in both roles. The ancient divisions between mental and manual laborers, between workplace controller and controlled, between bosses and wage slaves would be overcome, thereby achieving an immense step toward economic and hence social equality.

Building Support for the Cure

To win social approval for the creation and sustenance of WSDEs inside modern economies, a number of different campaigns could be pursued. A government program of financing and supporting new WSDEs could focus on the unemployed. FDR's model of federal job creation, for example, could be modified to provide specifically for the unemployed to regain work within self-directed enterprises. WSDEs would thereby become a significant kind of enterprise alongside traditional capitalist enterprises.

Another parallel campaign could stress the social benefits of giving citizens genuine freedom of choice between work within a traditional, hierarchical capitalist enterprise or within a workers' self-directed enterprise. That choice doesn't currently exist. This campaign would advocate extending government programs that assist small businesses and minority-owned businesses to include a major program for workers' self-directed enterprises. In such programs, government would provide subsidies, incentives, and technical support to particular kinds of enterprises, because markets dominated by capitalist enterprises would otherwise destroy them and because their existence provides important social benefits.

Still another campaign could be built around extending democracy from its currently very limited, residence-based, and mostly formal application to governing geographic areas. The basic idea would be to bring democracy to the communities that comprise worksites. Legislation, for example, might henceforth depend on the approval of both workplace democracies and residential democracies in a system of codetermination by both enterprise-based and residence-based democratic procedures. There are three compelling reasons to sustain such a campaign. First, no democracy is complete if it does not include the economy and its basic institutions. Second, the weakness and merely electoral formality of actually existing political democracies flow from their lack of economic democracy. Finally, the capitalist organization of production inside modern corporations directly contradicts and precludes economic democracy.

The problems of capitalism generally have been intensified and magnified by its recurring crises, especially now in the major downturn that began in 2007. Capitalism's problems have also become more visible to millions of people. As criticism mounts, so has oppositional thought and action. Capitalism is not "delivering the goods" to most people, and they know it. But we need to know why capitalism is in such deep trouble to see a way forward, to find a cure. I undertake the critical analysis and take an initial step forward in part I of this book.

Among the victims and critics of the capitalist system today, the fastest-growing demand is for a better alternative system. People are increasingly looking for changes in today's intertwined economic and political systems that can reasonably promise to do better than capitalism while avoiding the problems associated with earlier efforts to reform or replace it. Part II of this book focuses on clarifying what needs to be done and why. Most of this book, part III, is devoted to presenting, explaining, and endorsing what I believe to be the best alternative we have to accomplish what needs to be done.

Part I:
Capitalism in Deep Trouble

Capitalism has had an extraordinary run in the world—and nowhere more so than in the United States. Its celebrants demand, and capitalism as a system deserves, significant credit for catapulting Britain's former secondary colony, the United States, to its status as a global economic, political, and cultural superpower in two hundred years. The costs of the journey were huge and widely distributed; the gains were also huge, but less widely distributed. Here was a first sign of troubles to come. Moreover, a long-term rise in real wages bred conditions and expectations that eventually outran capitalism's capacities to sustain them. Here was another troubling sign. The former colony turned to immigration and imperialism as key means to further its ascendancy. Yet they also contributed to economic dependency on an evolving globalization of capitalism. This was another signpost.

Underlying and amplifying all of these problems were the basic structural flaws of the capitalist system. Its internal contradictions, tensions, and conflicts—ceaseless and unevenly developing antagonisms of labor and capital interwoven with the competitive struggles among capitalists—periodically generated downturns, crises, panics, and cyclical booms and busts. These were often moments of harsh but clear insight into the system's darker dimensions. Slowly, people accumulated not only appreciation of capitalism's profound social costs and many victims, but also increasingly powerful anticipations of economic and social systems that would be better than capitalism. Today, in the wake of one of capitalism's deepest and longest crises, critical insight has yet again been revived and sharpened. Today's critics can build on their accumulated understanding of capitalism's history and its present dilemmas.

Perhaps most importantly, the criticism of capitalism we can articulate today—as presented in part I of this book—allows us more clearly than ever to envision a genuinely new solution. That solution not only overcomes many of capitalism's flaws and failures, it also learns which misunderstandings and missteps to avoid from earlier efforts to go beyond capitalism. Together, the critique and the solution offer more hope for a breakthrough beyond a system in deep trouble than we have had at any point in the last half-century.

1 Capitalism and Crises

Like all important topics, capitalism has been defined and understood quite differently by different people and groups throughout its history. That fact requires everyone using the term to be clear and explicit about the particular definition being used. No one should proceed as if any one definition is the only one or is a definition on which everyone agrees.

For example, many contemporary usages of "capitalism"—in the media, among politicians, and in academic treatments—focus on two key dimensions. The first is private property: capitalism is a system in which the means of production (land, tools, equipment, raw materials) and products (goods and services) are privately owned by individuals and enterprises. They are not owned collectively by society as a whole or by the state apparatus (representing, at least in theory, society as a whole). The second dimension is the market: capitalism is a system in which productive resources and produced outputs are distributed by means of freely negotiated exchanges between their private owners. Distribution is not accomplished by means of the state's or any other collective agency's planned decisions. Thus, the twentieth century's great confrontation between "capitalism" and "socialism" was widely defined to be a struggle between private property and markets on the one hand and socialized property and government planning on the other.

I do not use that popular definition in this book. A full discussion of the different definitions of capitalism and of the disagreements among their adherents would take us far afield. Instead, I will underscore some problems with the popular definition as an introduction to the definition I use.

Private property is indeed a prevalent feature of capitalism. However, capitalist economies also typically contain significant amounts of productive property and products owned by state apparatuses in the name of the society as a whole. In the United States, for example, harbors, air space, transportation facilities, military equipment, large tracts of land, and many educational institutions are publicly owned.

Likewise, markets are common mechanisms of distribution, yet many capitalist economies also include the distribution of goods and services in nonmarket ways. In the United States, for example, food is distributed via food stamps issued to certain parts of the population, and many communities distribute park, fire, police, and school services to citizens based on local notions of citizens' needs, not on market exchanges. Inside most households, members produce all sorts of goods and services (cooked meals, cleaned clothes and rooms, repaired furniture, and so on) distributed to other household members according to traditional forms of household planning, barter, and exchange, not by means of market exchanges.

Moreover, private property and markets do not distinguish capitalist from other types of economic systems in human history. For example, the slaves in the noncapitalist economic system of the US South before the Civil War were private property. Similarly, in many parts of late medieval Europe, the land, horses, plows, and mills were often privately owned means of production, yet we refer to the economic system of that time as feudalism, not capitalism. Markets were also often features of slavery and feudalism as well as capitalism. For example, feudal lords often sold the products of their serfs' labor in markets; feudalism thus worked with a market system of distribution. Similarly, the cotton produced by slaves in the US South was regularly sold in world markets by means of exchange for money.

In short, private property and markets do not provide us with a clear demarcation between capitalism and, for example, slavery and feudalism as economic systems. Nor do we get much further if we try to deal with this problem by invoking individual "freedom." A commonly held view is that slaves lacked freedom because they were property and serfs lacked freedom because they were tied to their feudal manors, but workers in capitalism suffer neither of those forms of coercion. Among the problems with this definition is the fact that, under capitalism, wage workers are not free (other than formally, legalistically) because to live even minimally, they must work for others. They must sell their labor power to those who own the means of production in order to survive.

Because of these and many other difficulties, I define capitalism differently. My distinctive focus is not on property or distribution mechanisms or freedom. Instead, I highlight the internal organization of production and distribution: how the social sites where goods and services are produced and distributed organize those processes. A capitalist system is, then, one in which a mass of people—productive workers—interact with nature to fashion both means of production (tools, equipment, and raw materials) and final products for human consumption. They produce a total output larger than the portion of that output (wages) given back to them. The wage portion sustains the productive workers: it provides their consumption and secures their continued productive labor. The difference between their total output and their wage portion is called the "surplus," and it accrues to a different group of people, the employers of productive laborers: capitalists.

The capitalists receive the surplus from the productive laborers by virtue of a wage labor contract entered into between capitalist and worker. This wage labor contract specifies a particular commodity exchange. The capitalist agrees to buy—pay the worker regularly for—her or his labor time. The worker agrees to sell her or his labor time to the capitalist. The worker further typically agrees to use the tools, equipment, raw materials, and space provided by the capitalist. Finally, the worker agrees that the total output emerging from her or his labor is immediately and totally the private property of the capitalist.

The productive laborers—those who produce the surplus—use the wages paid to them by the capitalists to buy the goods and services they consume and to pay personal taxes. The capitalists use the surplus they obtain from their productive employees to reproduce the conditions that allow them to keep obtaining surpluses from their productive employees. For example, they use part of their surplus to hire supervisors to make sure the productive laborers work effectively. They use another part to pay taxes to a state apparatus that will, among other activities, enforce the contracts they have with their workers. They use yet another part of the surplus to sustain institutions (churches, schools, think tanks, advertising enterprises) that persuade workers and their families that this capitalist system is good, unalterable, and so on, so that it is accepted and perpetuated.

The workers who sign contracts with capitalist employers fall into two categories. Productive laborers are those directly engaged in the production of the goods and services that their employers sell; their labor yields the surplus that employers receive and distribute to reproduce their positions as capitalists. The term "unproductive laborers" refers to all those engaged in providing the needed context or "conditions of existence" for productive workers to generate surpluses. The unproductive laborers have their wages paid and their means of work provided by capitalists. The latter distribute parts of the surplus they get from productive laborers to pay and provide for the unproductive laborers.

In short, the capitalist economic system divides people into three basic economic groups: productive laborers, capitalists, and unproductive laborers. Just as the social context for the economic system—politics and culture—shapes and influences the economy, so the reverse also holds. To focus on a society's economic system, as this book does, does not mean that economics is any more important than politics, culture, or nature in the interaction among them that shapes every society. My focus on the capitalist economic system is driven chiefly by the widespread neglect of this dimension of today's social problems. One purpose of this book is to rectify that neglect.

For the last half-century, the capitalist economic system in the United States, and indeed in many other parts of the world, has gotten a free pass in terms of criticism and debate. Intense debates have swirled around other basic institutions or systems, such as marriage, schools, health care delivery, transportation, and urban structure.

Criticisms about their current conditions and problems have informed proposals for changes ranging from the relatively minor to the fundamental. However, our economic system—capitalism—has been almost entirely exempted from critical discussion, as if some taboo precludes criticism. Business and political leaders, the mainstream mass media, and the bulk of the academic community have substituted celebration and cheerleading for serious criticism and debate of capitalism. This was their response to the Cold War—and even more an intrinsic part of the conservative resurgence after the Great Depression, the New Deal, and the United States' wartime alliance with the Soviet Union frightened and galvanized such forces into reaction. They insistently treated capitalism as beyond criticism, debate, or basic change—and demanded no less of others.

During the postwar period, critics of capitalism were marginalized. Laws were passed that linked such criticism to disloyalty. Colleges and universities discriminated against such critics. Politicians competed in their adulations of capitalism and condemnations of all alternatives. Culture wars yielded purges of journalists, filmmakers, playwrights, and others suspected of sympathies with those who criticized capitalism as a system. The post-1940s history of the US labor union movement shows the stark social consequences of punishing critics of capitalism. First, the state apparatus pressed successfully for the systematic rooting out of those union leaders and activists who dared to include criticism of capitalism in their work. They were excoriated for advocating "subversive" and "ideological" politics rather than doing their proper jobs of "serving their members." Yet, as most unions fell into line, they also declined in part because of repeated attacks on unions as "special interests serving only their members" at the expense of the broader social good.

Criticism of particular capitalist enterprises or their particular practices did sometimes surface over the last half-century. It was possible to target capitalist enterprises' monopolistic activities, racial and gender discrimination, and environmental degradations—even their corruption of political institutions. However, critics learned to focus only on specific misbehaviors—not on the economic system that induced, rewarded, and reproduced them. Many oppositional movements foundered or collapsed because they excluded those who dared venture some criticism of capitalism as a system. By contrast, in 2011, the Occupy Wall Street movement broke with the traditional taboo, clearly affirming the legitimacy of criticizing capitalism itself.

Like any social system long exempted from criticism and debate, the capitalist system deteriorated behind its protective wall of celebration. Big business subordinated smaller capitalists when it did not overtake them. Laws protecting labor and labor unions were weakened, repealed, or simply not enforced. Freedom came to be redefined as first and foremost the freedom of businesses to decide what, where, and how to produce without interference from other parts of society. The results of so long-lasting a bar on serious criticism and debate of the capitalist system are many and sobering. They include the return to levels of inequality of wealth and income typical a century ago; consequent inequality in the distribution of political power and access to culture; atrophy of government-provided social services and supports; and multidimensional ecological crises.

In light of these developments, two central objectives of this book are to show how the severe crisis since 2007 is partly another result of capitalism and to help reopen the space for criticism of capitalism as a key step toward bringing about fundamental social change.

The capitalist economic system persists so long as labor contracts between capitalists and both productive and unproductive laborers provide acceptable quantities of surpluses to capitalists and employment and incomes to workers. Developments within the capitalist economic system and/or in its social and natural environment can disrupt—suddenly or gradually—the reproduction of the system. Then unemployed workers, unutilized means of production, and the resulting loss of output can coexist—often for years—in a stunning reproach to capitalism's pretensions to efficiency, equity, and progress.

Such disruptions are viewed by the masses of people in capitalist economies as "hard times" to be prepared for and endured. Capitalism's defenders fear disruptions as threats to the system. Capitalism's enemies treat them as opportunities for organizing people—especially workers—to change or supersede the system. No wonder then that capitalism has evolved mechanisms to avoid, evade, and respond to such disruptions.

Among these mechanisms have been government interventions that mix rescuing capitalists by direct subsidies (direct investments, loans, loan guarantees, below-market exchanges, and so forth), moderating mass suffering by providing state support to the unemployed and others, and passing regulations to reduce the most egregious economic practices aggravating the crisis. Simultaneously, ideological rationalizations of economic crises are expressed in claims that they weed out the inefficient enterprises and thereby strengthen the economic system. Finally, there are the bold assertions by politicians that newly enacted reforms and regulations will not only extricate society from its crisis but also prevent such crises from recurring.

1.1 Capitalism's Instability and Unevenness

Capitalism is a notoriously unstable economic system. Times of growth oscillate, often in extreme ways, with times of decline. This has always been the case since capitalism replaced feudalism in Europe and expanded globally from there. Its oscillations take many names, from downturns, busts, deflations, contractions, recessions, and depressions to upturns, booms, inflations, expansions, and prosperity. Professional economists have had to admit that capitalism displays endemic "business cycles" but keep hoping that something might be done to prevent them or at least to keep them from undermining the system. Many economists have built on the work of John Maynard Keynes to assert that the proper exercise of monetary and fiscal policies by government can realize that hope. Politicians have taken that assertion another step. In the United States, every president who presided over a cyclical downturn promised that his economic interventions (his mix of monetary and fiscal policies) would not only end that downturn but would ensure that we would not have another in the future. No politician or set of policies in the history of capitalism, however, has yet delivered on that promise.

Capitalism also develops unevenly across space—and always has. Thus, the growth of wealth in some parts of the world goes hand in hand with the growth of poverty in others. Every particular economic development path has its winners and its losers. Over the same period of time, employers often gain while—and often because—employees lose. This particular unevenness is a crucial cause of the global capitalist crisis that erupted in 2007, as I will demonstrate. Merchants and manufacturers developing in urban areas often produce simultaneous devastation in rural agricultural areas. The competitive success of one company in one town may devastate its rival companies and their towns. British capitalism's success was the root of India's crisis and decline. The explosive growth of capitalist enterprises in China finds its counterpart in devastated former manufacturing zones of the United States, much as earlier Europe's industrial revolution worked to undo production systems in Asia.

Capitalism's disruptions have always provoked complaints from those who suffer their results. Such complaints can and often have evolved into criticisms of capitalism as a system and from there to calls to usher in noncapitalist systems. The champions of the status quo sometimes respond with arguments that the causes of decline and underdevelopment are not the fault of capitalism, instead blaming natural conditions (for example, floods and droughts), political disruptions (such as wars and government intervention), or cultural patterns (inadequate entrepreneurship or savings behaviors) and so on.

The most common and enduring of these defensive arguments focuses on state economic intervention as the key external cause of capitalist crisis. Thus, for nearly a century now, it has been popular to blame capitalism's instability and unevenness on government interference in free-market economics. Economists, politicians, journalists, and pundits point to taxation, government spending, and regulation of markets as the culprits. The major counterargument—associated since the 1930s with Keynes—instead locates the root of capitalism's ups and downs in culture (how individuals cope with uncertainty about the future and their "propensities" to consume and save) and the ways in which culture and economy interact. Thus Keynes and those influenced by him see government economic intervention as useful and necessary to offset and to end the destabilizing interaction between culture and economics under capitalism.

Yet since capitalism's instability and unevenness are continually reproduced across every variation of external natural, political, and cultural conditions, some of those who defend the system have felt compelled to find better arguments that don't rely on external causes. These thinkers have sought to justify capitalism by insisting that its negative dimensions, such as cyclical downturns and inherent inequality, are simply the necessary price to be paid for economic and social progress. They claim that the gains of capitalism's winners are greater than the losses inevitably suffered by economic losers in the system, and therefore that instability and unevenness are ultimately—in terms of their net social effects—progressive. Capitalism is thus an efficient system, no matter how unstable and unequal.

Yet this notion of efficiency, much beloved by those who celebrate capitalism, is actually quite elusive. To know whether an economic system is efficient requires identifying and measuring all of its effects—the positive that accrue to the winners and the negative that affect its losers. Yet this is an impossible task. The problem is quite simply that the costs and benefits of capitalism at any time are infinite in number and project long into a future we can never know in advance. Besides the unsolvable problem of identifying and measuring all of capitalism's direct and indirect effects, we face an additional and insurmountable problem: whatever effects are identified and measured by an efficiency calculus are never the results only of capitalism as an economic system. That would be a grossly economistic, or economic determinist, claim. Those effects also have other causes (political, cultural, and natural) too numerous to identify or measure. In short, the notion of measuring the efficiency of economic events or processes or of an economic system is a mirage. It is not possible to identify or measure all of the effects of any social factor, nor is it possible to separate and weigh all the influences that combine to produce each effect. The very concept of efficiency would have been banished from discourse, let alone science, long ago if it had not proven so ideologically useful. Efficiency discourses resemble capitalist notions of efficiency, which in turn resemble the medieval doctrines and debates concerning how many angels can dance on the head of a pin: they too will one day strike people looking back as bizarre and absurd.

One particularly pervasive form of "efficiency" analysis, known as "cost-benefit analysis," claims to compare the total of benefits to the total of costs of any economic event or project and to then declare the system efficient if the total benefits exceed the total costs. It has become common across the history of capitalism for such calculations to serve those campaigning for nearly everything imaginable: a change in interest or tariff or tax rates; allowance to build a highway, housing development, or mall in place of a forest; regulation or deregulation of markets; and so on. Elaborate calculations of costs and benefits suitably dressed in charts and graphs have been key props in the efficiency theater that has provided ideological cover for the endless struggles attending capitalism's uneven development.

The usual winners in these struggles not only determine what economic event, plan, project, or system will prevail and its actual development path, they also wrap that path in the ideological mantle of "progress." However, capitalism's recurrent crises—and especially those that cut deep and endure for years—can and repeatedly do undermine the capitalist efficiency narratives of their times. The efficiency argument for capitalism rings hollow in the face of high and enduring unemployment affecting jobless millions and their relatives, friends, and neighbors. Watching the growing absurdity of foreclosures creating both homeless people and empty homes throws into serious question the standard defense of capitalist efficiency.

Yet the tradition of efficiency arguments for capitalism has taken such a hold in our discourse that even when capitalist crises have undermined them, claims regarding efficiency have often resurfaced in the rhetoric of anticapitalists. Socialists and communists during the Cold War often simply inverted the standard argument by insisting that it was socialism or communism that was efficient (or more efficient than capitalism) and thus represented progress. They, too, often ignored the impossibilities of identifying and measuring all costs and benefits and of separating and evaluating each of the myriad influences that produced them. Such socialists and communists also discovered that when social forces pushed against them strongly enough, their efficiency arguments no longer made sense. People became skeptical and eventually dismissive of those systems' claims to efficiency, much as happened to capitalism in its crises. The end of the communist governments in Eastern Europe toward the end of the twentieth century followed a mass loss of confidence in claims for socialism's greater efficiency compared to capitalism.

1.2 Welfare State Capitalism, 1945–1970s

In the wake of the Great Depression of the 1930s and World War II, both the United States and Europe turned dramatically from relatively laissez-faire to relatively state-interventionist forms of capitalism. State authorities in most countries limited the powers and wealth of corporations and enhanced the wages and state supports for the mass of people. State-interventionist capitalism "with a human face" replaced the more laissez-faire, harsher capitalism that had built up since the late nineteenth century.

From 1945 to the 1970s, state-interventionist capitalism was the norm, with Keynesian economics its dominant theoretical frame of reference. From the early 1970s until the crisis of the US economy in 2007, laissez-faire capitalism was the norm, supported by the widespread acceptance of a neoliberal ideological framework. The last half of the twentieth century was thus a perfect example of the shifts within capitalism between more and less state-interventionist phases.

In capitalism's current crisis, an ongoing struggle concerns the pace and form of the next possible oscillation. This time, however, the possibility of a break from capitalism's repeated oscillations to an altogether other economic system—different from both basic forms of capitalism—is stronger than it has been since at least the 1930s.

The extremes of wealth and poverty produced in the fifty years before 1929 generated a critical response. So, too, did the wrenching transformation of rural and agricultural people into an urban, industrial proletariat. Organized and militant trade unionism developed, as did large and militant socialist and then communist political parties. While their development was uneven, socialist and communist organizations were large, strong, and unified enough to become an important political force as the 1929 capitalist economic crisis deepened into a broader social crisis in many countries.

Thus, in the United States, for example, social movements led by socialists and communists transformed a rather conventional, centrist new Democratic president, Franklin D. Roosevelt, into an active promoter of massive state-interventionist capitalism. In the depths of the Great Depression he found himself caught politically between the conservative business leaders and the de facto alliance of the Congress of Industrial Organizations (CIO) and various socialist and communist parties. That alliance demanded immediate and massive government relief for the sufferings of average Americans brought about by the Great Depression. Militants within that alliance criticized capitalism as the cause of that suffering and openly called for its replacement.

Roosevelt's strategy took shape in this context. He maneuvered deftly toward his "New Deal," putting in place the basis for the form of welfare state capitalism that took hold in the United States from 1945 into the 1970s. To the masses and the union-leftist alliance, he offered the following bargain: if you give up your anticapitalist, revolutionary politics, I will provide legal protections for unions, political legitimacy for leftist parties (so long as they keep to certain bounds), and mass social welfare expenditures. Chief among the latter were the establishment of the Social Security system, the unemployment insurance program, and the direct hiring of more than twelve million new federal employees between 1934 and 1941. To the capitalists, he offered the following deal: if you give up significant portions of your personal and corporate incomes in the form of increased federal taxes to help pay for the federal government's new social welfare spending and if you accept the new legal protections for unions, I will provide labor peace and a left political alliance committed to reforms and collaboration with the government rather than revolution. Roosevelt warned the capitalists that failure to accept the deal he offered would mean having to cut a far less advantageous deal with the CIO–socialist–communist alliance then spreading quickly across the country.

Roosevelt's strategy succeeded. The struggle within the alliance between revolutionaries and reformers ended with the defeat of the anticapitalists. The coalition with Roosevelt and the Democratic Party around a reform agenda became the dominant politics of almost every section of the CIO–socialist–communist alliance (although some maintained, with much difficulty, revolutionary attitudes and goals). The capitalists were split. The portion that supported Roosevelt and his strategy was sufficient to win Roosevelt the political support he needed to carry through his major commitments to establish welfare-state capitalism. The other portion remained steadfastly opposed to his plans and immediately began massive agitation against the New Deal. When the capitalists opposed to welfare-state capitalism lost, they commenced their version of a long march to undermine and then undo the New Deal in the decades after 1945.

Roosevelt's reward for crafting the broad coalition was to become the most popular president in US history. He won four consecutive elections, prompting the Republicans to pass a law limiting all future presidents to two consecutive terms. He overcame the limits to his federal employment program when World War II enabled him to provide jobs to the remaining unemployed millions either as military personnel or in private enterprises producing for the military. The war, like the New Deal, provided some immediate benefits to employers and workers alike.

The cumulative traumas of depression and war from 1929 to 1945 profoundly shaped US history thereafter. Welfare-state capitalism commanded widespread political, ideological, and psychological commitments so vast and deep that it seemed this consensus could not be questioned, let alone overturned. However, its opponents were determined to do exactly that. On the one hand, they were deeply troubled by the growth of socialist, Marxist, and communist thinking and organizations across US society. The wartime alliance with the Soviet Union only deepened their concerns and fanned their paranoia.

The capitalist strategy of destroying the New Deal coalition became the prevailing theme of the postwar period, and served as prelude to undoing the welfare state it had achieved. The first major step was to break up the coalition by focusing attacks on the unions and the left political parties. The Taft-Hartley Act and the anticommunist witch hunts (of which McCarthyism was a part) were chief components of that first major step in the late 1940s and 1950s. An old political coalition was re-formed among capitalists, the Republican Party leadership, and various conservative religious, racist, regional, media, and patriotic organizations. This new right-wing coalition led the way to ending the wartime alliance with the Soviet Union as a key means to breaking up the New Deal coalition and thereby undoing the New Deal's achievements.

The New Right did not always win. It suffered some divisions and splits in the face of the African-American civil rights movement and the feminist movement. It also faced a broad cultural and political counterattack during the 1960s. Changing family conditions, attitudes, and sexual mores have repeatedly produced other splits. Yet the New Right found a substantial glue to hold itself together in a revival of the peculiar American tendency to demonize government as the ultimate cause of all social evils. By insisting that the cure for those evils requires only the removal or elimination of government's intrusions on individual freedom, various factions of the New Right could agree on attacking the government.

For capitalists, this worked beautifully. They found they could focus animosity on the welfare state bequeathed by the New Deal to postwar generations. This strategy involved demonizing unionists, socialists, communists, and a vast array of liberal reformers as undifferentiated proponents of state power, government intervention, bureaucracy, social engineering, and oppression. Each component of the New Right coalition found a way to define its goals in terms of opposing one state policy or another that it claimed was to blame for the particular problem it addressed.

After 1945, however, capitalists were generally much more successful than other members of the New Right coalition in achieving their goals. They were increasingly able to evade, weaken, or repeal New Deal laws and regulations. From 1945 to the 1970s, the rightist attacks took their tolls. The rightist coalition grew, winning more adherents especially among business and upper-income groups in response to such victories as the Taft-Hartley restrictions on labor unions and the shift in the burden of federal taxation from corporations to individuals and from upper-income individuals to middle-income groups. Meanwhile, defeats of the Democratic Party and defections—especially in the South—left many Democrats unwilling to defend New Deal programs. Tensions between the centrist and progressive wings of the party hardened into conflicts and splits. The New Left that arose in the 1960s was deeply critical of the Democrats as well as the Republicans.

The leftist surge of the late 1960s marked a major milestone in the demise of the New Deal legacy. On the one hand, it represented the protest—especially of younger Americans—against the long ideological and practical decline of that legacy. On the other hand, the right's reaction to the 1960s' resurgence of struggles culminated in the 1980 election of Ronald Reagan, a key indicator of shrinking working-class support for a Democratic Party that had proven itself incapable of inspiring much hope because it could not even protect, let alone advance, New Deal gains. Reagan's election also represented the right's renewed confidence and its determination to govern the next phase of US history.

The right-wing coalition's agenda largely dominated US politics from the late 1970s to the beginning of the 2007 recession. The Republican Party led the way and the dominant center of the Democratic Party followed, if less harshly and more slowly. Thus, the more progressive wing of the party (with its labor-union, African-American, student, and social-movement allies) became increasingly isolated and ineffective. The Democrats compromised on civil rights and liberties, sharpened already existing anti-Soviet and anticommunist foreign policies, and embraced neoliberal economic policies.

Much of the New Deal was systematically undone. Capitalism's previous swing, in the wake of the Great Depression, toward the hegemony of Keynesian economics, welfare statism, and social democracy gave way with Reagan's election to a rapid, sustained swing in the opposite direction. Reagan and British prime minister Margaret Thatcher rode this shift in capitalism back toward a relatively more laissez-faire, Anglo-American version of capitalism that came to acquire the name "neoliberalism." US and UK political leaders effectively reversed the post-1929 movement toward the more state-interventionist, social-democratic capitalism championed by the major continental European economies. Much as the Democratic Party in the United States hesitantly followed the Republican Party's rightward lurches, so European social democracy moved slowly in the direction of the US-UK model of capitalism. In both cases, the shifts continued even when loud rhetoric proclaimed otherwise. In much of the rest of the world, too, similar shifts were also under way.

These political developments coincided with surges in economic growth, profits as a percentage of national income, employers' overall profitability, and income and wealth gains disproportionately appropriated by upper-income groups. Much as the processes of laissez-faire capitalism had led to the crisis of 1929, so the processes of welfare-state capitalism built to its crisis in the 1970s.

1.3 Capitalism, 1970s–2007: The Crisis Building from Below

The 1970s brought to an end more than a century of rising average real wages in the United States. It had been a remarkable run for workers, unmatched by workers' experiences in any other capitalist country. US capitalism had been so profitable, its workers' rising productivity so steady, that capitalists could sustain capitalist growth by continuing to raise real wages in response to the US economy's major problem. That problem was a labor shortage. From the beginning of the colonial era, as arriving Europeans ethnically cleansed the native population, the profit possibilities of vast, fertile lands, good harbors, welcoming European markets, and a conducive climate were endangered by the problem of finding enough labor. Part of that problem was solved for the southern states by the slave trade. But a major part of the solution was wave after wave of European immigration.

Real wages higher than workers received or could anticipate in many parts of Europe and rising real wages were key to inducing European immigrants to journey to the United States. Not only were rising wages needed to entice immigrants, they were needed to keep them as wage-earners. Employers on the Eastern Seaboard understood that they needed to increase wages if they were going to keep workers from moving to the ample, nearly free lands of the US interior, where they might resume lives not so different from those of their European origins.

For more than a century before the 1970s, labor shortages were recurring problems, thus driving real-wage increases. The profitability of US capitalism enabled it to pay rising real wages. Employers benefited, though, from the fact that labor productivity grew even faster than real wages. This meant that profits rose, and the result was a century of dramatic US economic growth until the 1970s.

But in the 1970s, a set of broad economic changes ended the historic labor shortage just as US capitalism shifted to a relatively more laissez-faire phase. Real wages for US workers stopped rising. Wages, in real terms, have never had a sustained rise since the early 1970s. The fallout of this transformation in the US economy has been profound and contributed greatly to the crisis that began in 2007.

Real wages stopped rising because of changes on both sides of the labor market. Demand for workers declined in two major ways, while the supply of workers rose in two major ways. The demand for labor in the United States fell because the introduction of computers across the manufacturing and service industries in the 1970s and 1980s represented a sharp turn toward automation in the US economy. The demand for labor also fell because of the simultaneous movement of many manufacturing jobs out of the United States to locations where workers could be hired for far less. The export of US manufacturing jobs took off in the 1970s and 1980s, followed by the export of service sector jobs—so-called outsourcing—a trend that has continued into the present. Both of these economic developments were responses of US capitalism partly to a long period of rising real wages and partly to the postwar revival, by the 1970s, of real competitors to US capitalism, especially in Europe and Japan. Real-wage increases that once had been affordable became competitive liabilities, pushing US capitalists to seek profits as well as competitive advantages by substituting cheaper foreign workers for higher-wage domestic ones.

Just as these decreases in labor demands hit the US economy, two new groups of people were moving en masse into the US labor market in search of jobs. First were millions of adult women who were changing their self-definition and their lives. Often this happened through participation in the women's liberation movement, which became socially powerful and influential in the 1970s. No longer satisfied with traditional roles as wives, housekeepers, and providers of childcare and other unpaid household labor, many women sought full-time paid employment. The supply of labor surged as women entered the workforce by the millions. This development coincided with a new wave of immigration into the United States, this time mostly from Latin America, especially Mexico and Central America. Once again, capitalism's uneven development drove mass worker emigration from these areas—and, for many, the United States was the most attractive destination. Journalist Juan Gonzalez has called this immigration flow "the harvest of empire."

The North American Free Trade Agreement (NAFTA), which President Clinton signed in 1994, facilitated US-based multinationals' exports into and investments in Mexico. This destroyed the livelihoods of millions of Mexicans, especially farmers and small shopkeepers, who faced unspeakable economic hardship unless they emigrated. Mexico not only managed to export millions who no longer had decent job prospects in their native country, it also benefited from the massive cash inflow of remittances sent by Mexican workers in the United States back home to relatives and friends. NAFTA's benefits accrued to a tiny elite of Mexican employers, whereas its huge costs were more democratically distributed. These unequal consequences of NAFTA threatened major economic disaster for Mexico, which postponed it for a time thanks to the mass emigration and remittances mentioned above. After the next capitalist crisis hit in 2007, the housing industry dragged the whole US economy into a deep, prolonged downturn that cost millions of Mexican and other immigrants their jobs in the United States. They began returning to Mexico, and the remittance flow to Mexico decreased. What emigration had postponed for Mexico—coping with the disastrous consequences of uneven capitalist development and NAFTA—the 2007 crisis in the United States brought crashing back to an utterly unprepared country. Mexico quickly descended into social disintegration, marked by spiraling unemployment, the explosion of the drug industry, police and government corruption, and daily accounts of violent social decline.

Thus the combination of computerization, exported jobs, women surging into the labor market, and a new wave of immigration ended the period of rising real wages in the United States. Capitalists from Main Street to Wall Street quickly realized that employers could slow or stop wage increases, given that supply now exceeded demand in the labor market. Thus real wages today are roughly what they were more than thirty years ago.

The end of the long history of rising real wages in the United States has never received the public discussion and debate it merits. It has been traumatic for the working class. For decades, US workers and their families believed that hard work would yield a rising standard of living for the family and that each generation in this blessed land would live better than the one before. The so-called American Dream was within every working person's reach. Claims about "American exceptionalism" focused on everything but the historic labor shortage that drove rising standards of living. Politicians and pundits insisted that America's unique capitalism delivered a permanently rising standard of living to most workers because of a benevolent climate, a culture that favored entrepreneurship, civil freedoms, and even divine intervention.

Working-class parents promised themselves and their children better diets, clothing, housing, cars, appliances, educations, recreation and vacations, and other rewards. Until the 1970s, rising wages had enabled workers to afford to deliver on those promises. No wonder, then, that when real wages stopped rising no matter how hard one worked, workers were unwilling to give up on those promises.

Absent any national discussion of the changing labor markets and their social impact, US workers tended to blame themselves for the end of their rising real wages. They felt individually responsible for what was actually a social problem, an economy-wide set of changes.

Correspondingly, they sought individual responses ("solutions," they hoped) to what they believed were individual problems. If real wages per hour were no longer rising, then they would work more hours per week, take a second or even a third job, and encourage other members of the household to take on regular paid work. Millions of families pursued these strategies to cope with the changes in the economy. Women, who in the wake of the women's liberation movement had their own reasons to enter the workforce, found themselves under new pressure to seek paid employment. Since the stagnant wages of male workers alone could no longer support the American Dream, married families needed the addition of women's paid labor to provide needed household income. And over the next thirty years, women, especially in middle- and upper-income groups, moved steadily and massively into the paid labor markets. Most lower-income women had already been doing paid labor.

This post-1970 change in the conditions and lives of American women changed their families and households in ways that also altered US capitalism. Briefly, the mass movement of adult women, mostly married and with children, into paid, mostly full-time labor transformed households and families. Wives and mothers had long held disproportionate responsibility for maintaining the emotional integrity of the traditional nuclear family and the physical integrity of the traditional household. Even after those women undertook paid labor, they still performed the major share of the emotional and physical labor involved in shouldering those responsibilities, far more than their male partners. Women doing the "double shift" of workplace and household jobs simply could no longer devote the same time, energy, and attention to maintaining the emotional life of the family and the physical chores of the household as they had before adding paid work outside the household to their responsibilities.

Huge strains on families and households accumulated as a result of these changes. Divorce rates rose as tensions and strains within households mounted. Women brought their job stresses home; two incomes had to be jointly allocated and two sets of job-related expenses covered; children received less time and attention from parents. Women's former household labor, such as shopping, cooking, cleaning, and repairing clothes, appliances, and furniture, was increasingly replaced by purchasing substitute commodities (prepared meals, cleaning services, and disposable goods). Given the poor mass transit systems in the United States, when wives and mothers took paid jobs, families often needed to buy and maintain a second automobile. On US television programs, situation comedies changed from celebrating the happy nuclear and patriarchal family of the 1950s and 1960s to laughing with compassion at the increasingly dysfunctional families of the last several decades. A historically unprecedented and growing proportion of the population began choosing not to get married.

Flowing from these family and household changes, US consumption of all kinds of psychotropic drugs, legal and illegal, has soared. We became, in one revealing phrase, a "Prozac nation." Millions of family and household members felt acutely troubled that the support provided for them by traditional institutions seemed to be dissolving. Churches, synagogues, mosques, and the Republican Party, sometimes separately and sometimes together, found that by championing a "return to family values" they could very effectively draw new adherents.

The US economy adjusted to all these changes in family and household life, which were themselves consequences of earlier economic changes (above all, the end of rising real wages). The prepared-food and pharmaceutical industries boomed; so, too, did the women's clothing industry, which quickly discovered that women who took full-time paid work outside the home needed new wardrobes. The pornography industry grew fastest of all. As the manufacturing sector kept shrinking relative to the service sector, typically male-identified jobs declined relative to female-identified jobs. Men's real wages stagnated and became insufficient to yield the American Dream for their families and necessitated more women entering paid employment. The stresses and strains of all these changes made many men, raised with ideals of masculinity based on providing for their families, feel diminished, emasculated, and devalued. For many, pornography provided, in voyeuristic fantasy, the male control and domination that had eroded in their real lives.

Despite more hours of paid labor by more household members, the financial conditions of millions of households did not improve much. Women's entrance into paid labor added a set of new costs that absorbed a major part of their additional income. Paid childcare was far costlier than family members caring for children in the home. Prepared meals cost much more than raw food. A second car sharply increased household expenses, as did buying and cleaning women's workplace clothes for service-sector jobs. Household maintenance became increasingly a cost covered by cash outlays rather than the product of household members' labors. The higher education of daughters finally became as important a family consideration as that of sons, and that also meant higher household expenses.

US families discovered that doing more hours of paid labor and covering the associated extra costs left too little net income to offset the impact of stagnant real wages. The American Dream increasingly moved beyond working families' reach. Threatened with the prospect of slowing consumption, advertisers intensified their association of personal worth and success with the extent of one's consumption of commodities. Without rising real wages, and unable to earn enough with extra hours of labor, US households turned en masse to the only remaining way to achieve the American Dream: borrowing.

Mortgage debt soared, partly enabled by rising home prices and partly contributing to those rising home prices. More borrowing to buy homes increased demand for them and, thus, their prices. As prices rose, homeowners could refinance and borrow more against the increased collateral their rising home values represented. This wonderful "virtuous circle" yielded a housing expansion that fueled an economic upturn. When the Federal Reserve, anxious about a recession after September 11, 2001, lowered interest rates quickly and sharply, the housing expansion became a housing bubble. When that broke in 2007, the virtuous circle turned into a vicious circle of falling housing prices, reinforcing declines in mortgage credit and rising rates of home foreclosures that further depressed housing prices. The housing industry's depression from 2008 onwards has been a major cause of the depth and duration of the economic crisis, making it the worst since the Great Depression of the 1930s.

Other forms of personal debt skyrocketed as well. The credit card was transformed in the 1970s from a non-debt-accumulating convenience for business and elite travelers to a debt-accumulating necessity for nearly everyone. As working families more often needed two cars to enable multiple members to undertake paid work, auto loans became important components of household debt. Finally, higher education for multiple children—deemed a necessity for future job and income prospects—attached mounting levels of debt to students. Unprecedentedly high and rising consumer debt in all these forms became a basic fixture of the US economy in the new millennium. Widely quoted statistics showed that when the Great Depression hit in 1929, the average US family had debts roughly equal to 30 percent of its annual income. In 2007, according to the Federal Reserve, the comparable number was well over 100 percent.

Across the 1980s and 1990s and up to 2007, US families worked and borrowed more and more, while real wages stagnated. Workers experienced physical exhaustion from added paid labor, emotional and psychological stresses from changing labor and gender roles, and mounting anxiety about accumulating levels of debt that could not be sustained. This mix of working-class responses to the end of rising real wages postponed the national reckoning with the significance, implications, and social costs of this historic shift. However, when households could no longer manage the costs of this postponement—when they began defaulting on their debts—the system crashed. Even so, despite repeated claims to the contrary, the crash was not primarily caused by a working class that could no longer earn, borrow, or spend more, as I will explain.

1.4 Capitalism, 1970s–2007: The Crisis Building from Above

While household debts and the housing bubble had indeed become unsustainable, the crash resulted largely from the huge financial speculation that employers, top executives, and professionals had built up on the foundation of consumer debt. The mechanism here was straightforward. First, banks packaged consumer debts (mortgages, credit card debt, auto loans, and student loans) into a new kind of financial investment: asset-backed securities (ABS). Where regular stocks and bonds were investments in and thus claims on companies that produced goods or services, ABS were different.

ABS gave those who bought them a claim on the principal or interest payments of consumer loans. Those who invested in ABS received in return a portion of the regular flow of consumers' payments servicing their debts. Successful businesses were among the main investors in ABS and derivative financial instruments associated with them.

To understand where ABS investors found the money to invest in and thereby fuel the explosion of ABS leading up to the crash of 2007, I will briefly explore yet another consequence of the stagnation of real wages since the 1970s. While real wages stayed flat, worker productivity rose steadily over the same period. Workers in the United States were better educated, worked with more and better machines (thanks largely to computerization), and worked harder and faster over those years. They steadily produced more output in goods and services per hour, year after year. Meanwhile, their employers did not pay them higher real wages in exchange for their higher productivity or output. As a result, the gap grew between what employers paid workers per hour and what workers produced for their employers per hour. That gap showed up as expanding employer profits. Since real wages stayed flat as productivity kept rising, profits kept climbing. This profit scenario in turn prompted a record-setting peacetime boom of the stock market. The top executives of US corporations, the smaller businesses and professionals who served them, and the owners of stocks in those enterprises became very wealthy. A culture developed in which the rich competed in terms of lavish lifestyles but also in terms of finding profitable investments for their accumulating financial wealth. Hedge funds proliferated as businesses focused on helping the newly rich find profitable investments to become yet richer. One major new profitable investment they promoted was ABS and their associated derivatives.

So now, by following the money, we can grasp the economic interconnections that drove world capitalism into crisis. First, stagnant real wages and rising productivity sharply altered the distribution of income and wealth in favor of profits and increases in wealth for the rich. Second, the working class responded by borrowing vast sums to postpone the end of rising consumption that would have had been necessary if they relied only on their wages. Third, employers and the rich lent back to the workers, via ABS, a portion of the extra profits they made from real-wage stagnation. For thirty years, these interconnections generated enough gains—in the forms of rising debt-based consumption for the masses and rising wealth for the employers and the rich—to reproduce the system. But the pattern was unsustainable.

A pyramid of speculations was erected on ABS—as ever more profit-based incomes piled into them—and on their allied financial instruments, such as the peculiar ABS insurance policies called credit default swaps (CDS). Hedge funds and banks took ever-greater risks as they competed for high returns to lure investments from those who kept accumulating profits. Alongside rising investor risks, workers' rising debt levels combined with stagnant real wages to erode their capacity to service their debts. When this capacity was exhausted, growing numbers of workers defaulted on their debt obligations. So did the major banks and many of those who had issued and owned ABS, CDS, and other speculative instruments tied directly or indirectly to the values of workers' debts. Very quickly, the capital markets, increasingly interconnected across the world by the previous decades of globalization, spread the impact of the US credit collapse internationally. Financial markets had marketed toxic ABS, CDS, and related investments around the globe—and in the process facilitated the globalization of the crisis when it hit.

1.5 A Digression on What or Whom to Blame

Capitalism drives workers and capitalists to play the roles assigned to them by the system. No matter how rigged the system, individual players seek to reap the system's rewards and avoid its penalties, to take the necessary risks and pay the necessary costs to enjoy its benefits. Capitalism also assigns the state its role in supporting and undergirding certain activities, regulating other activities, and preventing certain excesses. State officials perform these functions just as workers and employers perform theirs.

Did some state officials perform badly or become corrupt prior to the 2007 crash? No doubt, but that has been true both in capitalism's upswings and downswings. Because of the durability and social influences of anti-statism on the right and left, many have been tempted to attack some or all state institutions or officials (or state-private partnership institutions and officials). Rightists see in the state's activities the roots of most evils, including cycles and crises. The Nobel laureate and economist Milton Friedman, for example, blamed the Great Depression on political intervention in "free markets" by the government. Republicans often claim that Democrats in Congress or the White House spend and borrow excessively, causing deficits and economic downturns. By contrast, leftists usually target one part or another of the state and especially state-private institutions. For example, one favorite target of the left (and of the right as well) has been the Federal Reserve system, which many accuse of mismanaging the monetary system in favor of bankers, contributing to economic crises and unjust governmental bailouts. Democrats likewise blame Republicans in Congress or the White House for failing to grasp Keynesian insights, failing to undertake countercyclical deficit spending, and thereby worsening and prolonging economic crises and their massive social costs. The Nobel laureate and economist Paul Krugman analyzes the US and European governments' responses to the post-2007 capitalist crisis in just such terms.

These arguments on the left and right are peculiar. We are asked to believe that different parts of the state apparatus and different subgroups of state officials work to undermine the capitalist system. Were they not created within and continuously shaped by the capitalist system in ways that celebrated and justified reproducing that system? Somehow, in these arguments, the behavior of state institutions and officials disrupted the smooth, noncyclical reproduction of capitalism. Otherwise our behavior would have accomplished just that reproduction.

In this view, private businesses and individuals respond appropriately and successfully to the signals, risks, and rewards of capitalism, whereas the state does not. Yet state interventions in capitalist economies were crucial to their beginnings and early growth, have been continuous ever since, and, over the longer historical span, have mostly grown, absolutely and relatively. At the same time, this focus on the state as the rogue, disruptive part of the entire system has long attracted those who, for various reasons, cannot bear to question, criticize, or even debate changing the capitalist system as a whole.

"Criminals" are another rogue actor blamed for capitalism's cycles. The mass media and appropriate authorities routinely denounce those illegally gaming the system: the underpaid secretary who embezzles, the insider trader who makes illegal profits, the syndicates that run whole industries or cities. Such illegal economic activities happen all the time, even more so during crises. Criminal activities are thus more effects than causes of capitalism's cycles. Yet historical and contemporary records overflow with blame variously heaped on the illegal acts of financiers, corporate executives, corrupt state officials, union leaders, and "organized crime" for causing capitalism's cycles and crises.

Whether consciously or not, such a focus on misbehavior by the state or by criminals serves to avoid blaming the system and its rules and regulations, its structure of rewards and penalties. Pinpointing "the bad guys" perpetuates the ancient art of scapegoating, deflecting blame on convenient targets when in fact the system is the problem.

◆ ◆ ◆

Everyone, individual or business, ever blamed for contributing to capitalism's recurring crises has defended their actions by explaining that they were just participating in the economic system, responding to its signals, and trying to succeed. For centuries, in every capitalist country, individual economic actors have been charged, convicted, and imprisoned for violating some law, and businesses have been shut down or sanctioned for similar reasons. But the individuals and businesses that follow sooner or later replicate their behavior. For example, from long before Charles Dickens's 1857 novel *Little Dorrit* all the way up through the stunning multibillion-dollar scam of Bernard Madoff, Ponzi schemes have recurred across capitalism's history. Capitalism produced these schemes, which only grew larger as the system expanded. The slave and feudal systems that preceded capitalism fostered forms of crime rooted in their mixes of economic risks and rewards. But those systems never displayed the recurring boom-and-bust cycles common to all forms of capitalism. These cycles are the product of capitalism—not of this or that group (the state, criminals, others) functioning within that system and in response to its upswings and downswings. Capitalist societies can continue to monitor, identify, regulate, and prosecute economic misdeeds, but doing so never will prevent cycles and crises. It never has. Overcoming the systemic roots and nature of capitalist crises requires a change in the economic system.

2 Crisis and Government Response

I have attached no dates to this chapter's title. That is because the government response to the crisis that hit US capitalism in 2007 will continue for many years to come. The social and economic consequences and costs of such long-lasting crises extend deeply and widely into a society's future. The impoverished families of the long-term unemployed strained to the point of dysfunction, communities deprived of viable economies, interrupted educations, lost skills: these and many more results of capitalism's crisis will put difficult demands on governments for years. On the one hand, they will aggravate social problems that impose costs on governments. On the other hand, affected individuals and businesses will pay less in taxes to fund local, state, and federal governments. We will all be paying the heavy costs of capitalist crises both directly in our personal lives and indirectly through declining government services and protections.

Nonetheless, it is instructive to study the first few years of the US government's response as the economic downturn gathered speed and force in early 2008 and then intensified into full-fledged collapse between September 2008 and April 2009. The collapse occurred most dramatically in the credit system, where it took the form of a credit freeze—lending stopped. It had become clearer in 2008 that the number of mortgages that could no longer be serviced by borrowers was larger and growing faster than had been expected. Therefore, the owners of mortgage-backed securities (MBS) and other asset-backed securities (ABS) faced not only their declining values but also great uncertainty about what price they might fetch if and when a holder tried to sell them to anyone else. Uncertainty can destabilize markets even more than rapid price declines. Two huge investment banks, long active in the MBS market and large owners of MBS, collapsed in 2008. Bear Stearns was forced into a massively discounted handover of its assets to JPMorgan Chase, and Lehman Brothers was forced to declare bankruptcy. Their creditors, fearing the implications of the declining values of such investment banks' ABS assets, demanded repayment of their loans and in other cases said they would not renew loans that were coming due. The investment banks could not manage or survive the loan stoppage they faced because of the declining values and prospects of their ABS holdings.

These dramatic events, among others that received less publicity, sufficed to freeze credit markets by autumn 2008. Few banks could or would lend to others because every bank knew that other banks held unknown amounts of asset-backed securities whose values were falling, uncertain, or both. To lend to any bank—even overnight—meant risking being told the next morning, week, or month that the borrowing bank could not repay because its ABS values were collapsing and its access to credit had vanished. Other financial enterprises were likewise drawn into the credit freeze. Some held ABS or depended on banks that did. Others had hedged their holdings of ABS—as many banks did—by purchasing credit default swaps (CDS) as insurance against the defaults that were proliferating in 2008 and 2009. Still others had found new profit opportunities by speculating in CDS themselves, since CDS values rose (mostly) and fell (sometimes) as rumors swirled about ABS insured by those CDS.

Yet another shock took the credit markets over the edge as they were hit by a three-part punch. As the crisis spread, it emerged, first, that owners of ABS who had purchased CDS as insurance to cover default risks were turning to the issuers of those CDS to cash in on that coverage. It next became clear that one of the world's largest issuers of CDS was the largest insurance company in the world, American International Group (AIG), and that while AIG had profited greatly from premiums it earned by selling CDS, it had not accumulated the reserves needed to pay the claims arriving in 2008 from those holding AIG's CDS. When this news spread, it further destroyed the values of both CDS and ABS. Credit then stopped flowing throughout a global capitalism that had, over the previous thirty years, come to lubricate ever more transactions of daily life with credit. More and more personal and business activities required and entailed loans. Capitalist countries had all become credit-dependent nations, if not yet all "credit card nations." Governments, enterprises, and especially the public had been borrowing at growing rates; in the previous chapter, I explored the reasons for growing personal debt. But the intertwined phenomena of competitive globalization and mergers and acquisitions led the corporate sector into massive debts as well. Finally, governments across the world had increasingly run deficits and thereby accumulated national debts in managing the contradictions of capitalist economies.

The credit freeze posed a fundamental threat to a global capitalism dependent on global credit availability. This became clear first and most immediately in the United States, the center of the global markets in ABS and CDS. Some way had to be found—and fast—to unfreeze the credit markets. Otherwise, their freeze would be quickly transmitted by a globalized market system and disrupt the production and distribution of goods and services around the world. The tremor of an impending general capitalist collapse radiated out from its epicenter in New York.

2.1 The Bailouts and Federal Budget Deficits

The US government's first step to bail out its major corporations and unfreeze credit markets was the Troubled Asset Relief Program (TARP), created by Congress and President Bush in October 2008. That legislation provided $700 billion for the Treasury to use chiefly in two ways. The first entailed buying "troubled assets"—ABS and especially badly depressed MBS—from banks and other financial institutions. These assets, often with depressed, falling, or uncertain value, were thus removed from the balance sheets of private financial enterprises and added to the balance sheet of the federal government. The second major use of TARP money was for buying special (usually nonvoting) shares in banks and other corporations such as General Motors, AIG, and Citigroup. The purpose of these purchases was to enlarge the capital reserves of these corporations so that they would be more creditworthy and thus better able to obtain loans. A very small portion of funds went to the Making Home Affordable Program, which was introduced by the Obama administration in 2009 to assist homeowners facing foreclosures. However, this program was never well-funded or successful.

TARP was a classic example of trickle-down economics: priming the pump mostly at the top of the economic pyramid in the hope that the resulting flow might trickle down to everyone else and thereby overcome the economic downturn. But the expected trickle failed to materialize. Calls for banks to use their government assistance to renew lending to small and medium-sized businesses and to individuals went unheeded. Bank spokespersons explained that imprudent lending had gotten them into the crisis and they were not about to repeat that mistake. In short, the credit freeze was alleviated at the top of the credit system, but not enough to stop or reverse the downturn. The US economy went from bad to worse in the last months of 2008 and the early months of 2009. Republicans and Democrats alike had agreed to try to deal with the deepening economic crisis by spending lavishly on stimulus programs but not taxing anyone to pay for them. Instead the Treasury Department borrowed heavily—as usual, chiefly from banks, insurance companies, rich people, and foreign governments—and the national debt surged.

Bush and Obama, Republicans and Democrats, all pursued and approved a government spending program financed by deficits. However, the November 2010 midterm election results strengthened Republicans, as the right-wing Tea Party movement capitalized on growing popular discontent over economic problems and pressed its audience to vote Republican. The Republican Party led an intense, across-the-board opposition to Obama and his policies. Conservative forces attacked the fast-growing national debt and large current account deficits as the root problem, rediscovering classic arguments that cast them as dangerous burdens threatening to require future tax increases. Such arguments treated deficits as failures of the Obama administration rather than products of a capitalist crisis. Further government outlays that required deficit spending thus became ever harder to pass in Congress.

Of course, stimulus programs could have been financed by taxation. It would have made good economic sense to tax corporations and the richest individuals—especially given that the impact on their spending would likely have been minimal—and spend the revenues on Washington's large budget deficits. Working and poor people would have spent the great part of any such stimulus money and thereby significantly multiplied its positive economic effects. Instead, corporations accumulated huge cash hoards, since spending on investment or growth made no sense in a depressed, declining economy. Likewise, the rich, who had become relatively much richer over the previous thirty years, spent little of their income in a down economy.

In short, taxing these nonspenders and using the revenues to spend on economic stimulus programs would have been a classic anti-crisis program—and such a robust tax-based stimulus program would incur little or no budget deficit and thus a lower increase in the national debt, if any. But neither Republicans nor most Democrats dared move in that direction for fear of alienating the corporations and the rich. After thirty years of skyrocketing corporate profits (especially for large corporations), during which the top 1 percent of income earners had become much richer relative to the other 99 percent, major parties and politicians had become much more dependent on the financial support of those two groups than ever before. Workers' stagnant wages, coupled with the extra hours of household members' labor and the anxieties of rising individual debt, had combined to sharply lessen mass participation—and even interest—in politics. Meanwhile, growing income and wealth inequality motivated corporations and the rich to use their enhanced resources to shape politics so that government would protect their new financial gains from the envy, resentment, and demands of the 99 percent.

Remarkably, no proposal to fund the bulk of federal stimulus spending by taxing corporations or the rich was ever seriously entertained by either party. No programs for social welfare spending or federal job creation—like those enacted during FDR's New Deal—were ever seriously debated, let alone passed. The economic model that led to growing income and wealth inequalities and caused the crisis had so captured the two-party political system that it was incapable of mobilizing sufficient fiscal stimulus to reverse or even stop the unfolding economic decline.

Political dysfunction aggravated economic dysfunction. As this became clear, an increasing number of people began to question the system as a whole—the social combination of such an economy and such a politics. When the crisis persisted in the years after 2008, conventionally partisan criticisms of this or that aspect of the system gave way to criticism of the entire system. The right, as usual, blamed poor people for taking out loans they could not afford and government economic policies for blocking or distorting what would otherwise have been a smoothly growing and profitable private enterprise market capitalism. The left, as usual, blamed greedy financial and other corporate interests—and insufficient government regulation of them—for the economic crisis. But a significant and growing constituency rejected efforts to blame the parts in favor of questioning the whole. The system was the problem. More people came to feel that the economic crisis was endemic to the capitalist system, part of its normal mode of operation.

2.2 The Bailouts and the National Debt

In capitalist economies, governments are often caught between the demands of assertive coalitions of business and the richest citizens and the demands of the mass of the people. In the United States since the 1970s, such business coalitions had successfully obtained extensive government services and supports while simultaneously reducing their federal tax burdens and regulations. The burden of taxation was increasingly shifted onto the working classes (called "middle classes" in the United States). For example, whereas federal taxes on business had brought in far more than taxes on individuals in the 1940s, by the first decade of this century, that relationship had been starkly reversed: federal taxes on businesses brought in a quarter of the tax revenues collected from individuals. And whereas in the 1950s and 1960s, the richest US individuals faced a top income tax rate of 91 percent, repeated declines brought the top bracket to 35 percent by the first decade of this century. The fastest-growing federal revenue source during these years was not the less and less progressive individual income tax, but the regressive Social Security and Medicare taxes. In the simplest terms, corporations and the rich partly utilized the explosion in profits that began in the late 1970s to wield enough political power, in ways explained below, to shift the federal tax burden from themselves onto the "middle classes."

The framework and rationale for this remarkable shift of the federal tax burden was neoliberalism. In more common language, the tax-shifting maneuvers were promoted as "job-creation" policies.

With fewer taxes to pay, corporations would expand and rich individuals would invest: twin sources of more jobs. This theoretical argument is weak, however. Many other factors combine to determine whether and how much corporate or individual income saved from taxes will be spent on growth and investment. The empirical argument is weaker still: for every example of tax reduction encouraging job growth, counterexamples illustrate the opposite. Nonetheless, justified as creating jobs, tax reductions on the corporations and the rich occurred repeatedly and dramatically throughout the last thirty years. This was less because corporations and the rich wanted them—nothing new there—than because mass working-class opposition was not sufficiently mobilized to prevent them.

To explain how and why the political forces led to that outcome, I will begin by noting how corporations and the rich used their rising profits and their falling tax burdens to shape politics. As they altered the tax system to their advantage, they worked hard to define "the tax issue" politically as having nothing to do with shifting burdens from one social group to another. Politicians and politically motivated think tanks inundated public discourse with affirmations that all taxes were excessive burdens that sustained wasteful bureaucrats. Government employees did much that was useless or worse. Above all, they argued, government assistance sustained people who thereby avoided work or lost whatever work ethic they ever had. Costly and wasteful dependence on state support—and hence ultimately on taxes—replaced productive labor in private enterprises. Worse still, those who did work, the working classes, had to pay ever more taxes to support those on state support who did not. Likewise, taxes on corporations and the rich supported those who did not work while dampening and discouraging the corporate expansion and private investment that created jobs.

Corporations and the rich—through the political statements and actions of the Republicans and Democrats (the latter less enthusiastically because of their historic ties with the working classes)—became loud advocates of cutting taxes and wasteful, counterproductive government "welfare spending." This would be the best policy for everyone. Politicians became advocates of restrained federal spending, balanced budgets, fiscal conservatism, and so on. Well-publicized and corporate-funded "popular tax revolts" organized people around the demand for general "tax relief," such as the California bill proposed by Governor Gray Davis and passed in 1999, which was copied in many other states. Corporations and the rich funded political allies who made sure that tax cuts went mostly to them.

The pursuit of these politics had many detrimental outcomes. Reduced government tax revenues raise the question of what to do about the expenditure side of the federal budget. With lower tax revenue, Washington could more easily justify cutting social welfare spending. However, the groups calling for less government spending always encountered a daunting problem that often enraged them and strained their political relationships: the interests of many corporations and rich people in US capitalism are served by and depend on federal supports and spending. These beneficiaries fiercely protect the federal spending they want by using their profits and personal wealth to that end. Such beneficiaries include the military-industrial complex, energy companies, transportation companies, the health care industry (a complex composed of doctors, hospitals, pharmaceutical companies, and medical insurance providers, among others), agribusiness, and many other commercial interests. Such groups also oppose cutting various kinds of social spending when they fear employees might successfully secure higher wages and salaries to offset such cuts.

The working class also resists federal spending cuts upon which it relies: Social Security, Medicare, and Medicaid benefits, federal employee pay and benefits, federal aid to state and local public service budgets, student loan funds, and so on. Many in the working class want lower federal taxes, but without cuts in important areas of federal spending. Because the working class has for many years lacked the organization that might mobilize funds sufficient to compete with the profits and personal wealth that corporations and the rich use to buy political influence, it wields its influence in a disorganized and generally less effective way: through voting. Workers support candidates they perceive as being committed to lowering the overall tax burden without lowering the widespread benefits of federal spending.

The two sides place contradictory demands on the federal government and politicians elected to federal offices, who have responded by repeatedly cutting taxes on corporations and the rich, especially—but also, to a far lesser degree, on the working class. Parties and politicians thereby reward the financial contributions of corporations and the rich and the votes of the working class. Likewise, to the same end, they tend to avoid spending cuts that could risk alienating their financial supporters or voting constituents. Of course, sometimes the parties and politicians cannot navigate the contradiction without offending one group or the other by raising a tax or cutting a government outlay. However, that is widely recognized as a dangerous situation. Such moves have often ended political careers, serving as an object lesson to party leaders and elected officials that the far better political strategy is to find a way to both keep taxes down and government spending up.

The only way to accomplish this "resolution" of the contradictions capitalism imposes on the federal budget is deficit spending.

The federal government must borrow if it is to sustain (or raise) federal expenditures while cutting (or not raising) federal taxes. Federal borrowing was, before the 1980s, a more exceptional practice, necessitated chiefly by wars and largely repaid thereafter. During the Great Depression, the Roosevelt administration championed deficit spending in a new way, as a key device in overcoming and reducing the social pain of major economic downturns. The work of Keynes defined deficit spending as an appropriate countercyclical fiscal policy—but deemed such deficits exceptional and thought they should be repaid once an economic downturn had given way to an upturn.

After 1980, it became routine practice to expand federal deficits and thus also the national debt in the United States and many other countries. Thus, when the major capitalist downturn hit in 2007 and continued for years, the federal government's sudden, large counter-cyclical spending imposed big deficits and big increases on an already-elevated US national debt. The severity and urgency of the 2008 and 2009 economic crises and the resurgence of Keynesian economics combined to encourage and justify all the government borrowing. However, debt levels that had been rising since the 1970s, coupled with the post-2007 explosion in additional debt, raised a new problem for capitalism internationally.

The major public lenders to borrowing governments were banks, insurance companies, large corporations, and wealthy individuals, as well as other cash-rich national governments. By 2010, these lenders were becoming concerned that the debt levels of the borrowing governments were becoming "dangerous," lest they find taxpayers unwilling to pay the additional taxes or forego public services and jobs to free up the money to service such crisis-driven debt increases.

This accumulating set of contradictions led to a capitalist crisis of historic proportions that has persisted for years after its beginnings in 2007. Wage, productivity, and profit shifts, as well as income and wealth distribution movements and credit market developments, coalesced into a toxic mix of economic disruptions. The massive deficit spending with which the US government responded now generated yet another contradiction. Its policy decision to concentrate on unfreezing the credit markets as the key to overcoming the crisis meant that the government bailed out many of the largest private financial enterprises. Once these enterprises were again able to lend—because of the federal government's help—they proved very hesitant to lend again, lest they risk another financial meltdown. They preferred to lend only to the biggest and safest possible borrowers.

This hobbled credit for all sorts of small, medium-sized, and endangered businesses and for many debt-laden consumers, thereby undermining any general economic recovery. It also hobbled credit for the many governments indebted to these lenders. The starkest case was Greece, but many other countries, including Portugal, Spain, Italy, Hungary, and Ireland, experienced similar credit problems. Lenders enjoyed a lenders' market as governments desperate to borrow in order to soften or offset the crisis besieged them for loans. Greece, a relatively poor and small country, already had an indebted government when the crisis imposed further borrowing, making it not the best credit risk. At the same time, Greece had perhaps the most organized and militant labor unions and left political parties in Europe. As the elections of 2012 showed, they might well block any Greek government's plans for servicing debt at the expense of raised domestic taxes, reduced domestic public services, or both.

Because lenders preferred to lend to the relatively much more secure US or German governments than to the Greek government, borrowing costs in Greece rose sharply. What the Greek government might have done to stimulate demand and otherwise counter the impact of the global crisis on its country was prevented by the need to devote scarce public resources to paying lenders. Worse still, raising taxes and cutting government jobs and services to get the money to pay creditors only caused Greek economic conditions to deteriorate further. This, in turn, reduced government revenues, requiring more borrowing in a vicious downward slide into economic catastrophe. Since a large portion of the Greek government's debts were held by non-Greek banks, rising debt costs drained wealth out of Greece altogether. For years the world watched as a small, poor corner of the European economy foretold a possible future for many other heavily indebted governments reeling from the twists and turns of the capitalist crisis.

All of these developments give a new importance and currency to the term austerity. Austerity means a combination of higher taxes and other payments flowing from the population to the government, and fewer jobs and services provided by that government to its constituents. It is rationalized as the necessary "medicine" to cure the "illness" of costly national debt. The nearly universal practice of governments in capitalist countries for the previous thirty years has now been reconceptualized as a policy error that caused an economic sickness. Austerity has become the prescription for countries to regain economic health.

The crisis of capitalism since 2007 was pushed into the background, denied a role as a key cause in nations' economic problems. No discussions in the establishment media focused on systemic alternatives to capitalism that might solve or remove the problem of regularly recurring crises, instead presenting the trickle-down responses of governments as if no alternative responses were possible or worth considering. Instead, the big problem of the day became the sickness of government deficits and debts. And the appropriate—if painful—medicine was austerity. Republicans and Democrats argued chiefly over the details of austerity: its size and timing, the precise mix of tax increases and spending cutbacks, and so on. Most Republicans preferred tax cuts for business and the rich (versus average citizens) more than most Democrats, and most Republicans preferred cutting government employment and social welfare services more than most Democrats. But both agreed on far more than they disagreed on.

Meanwhile, lenders everywhere sharply scrutinized and ranked the risks of government borrowers. As lenders imposed or threatened to impose rising loan costs, those governments scrambled to prove that they represented no significant risk for lenders. They did this by demonstrating their political capacity to impose austerity programs on their people and to free the money needed to service their present debts and any future debts. This meant showing that they could indeed raise taxes and cut public employment and services to raise funds. Politicians claimed that an effective dose of austerity now could restore lenders' confidence, thereby allowing them to avoid a much larger dose of austerity later. Thus the Greek socialist government of George Papandreou, which had come to power in 2009 on a platform opposed to the injustice of austerity, reversed its position. It justified austerity to its Greek constituents on the grounds that not imposing it would necessarily mean worse cuts later. Critics of austerity programs in Greece and elsewhere countered that austerity now would cause further economic decline, depress tax revenues, and worsen deficits, thus paving the way for still-harsher austerity programs later.

In fact, US history gives the lie to the entire austerity discourse. Austerity programs are far from the only or the best policies for coping with capitalist crises. During the Great Depression of the 1930s, when unemployment was much higher than during the current crisis and federal tax revenues had fallen relatively more, the policy solution was to increase state spending sharply: the opposite of today's typical austerity programs. FDR's administration established Social Security, unemployment insurance, and a federal jobs program that hired many millions of the unemployed. At the same time, this social spending surge was not paid for by a corresponding burst of federal borrowing on the scale of what happened after 2007. Instead, FDR imposed heavy taxation on businesses and on rich individuals. This helped to finance the fiscal stimulus for the bottom—a kind of trickle-up economics—without exclusive dependence on fast-rising government debt.

The strengths and weaknesses of FDR's response to capitalist crisis and the strengths and weaknesses of the crisis responses deployed since 2007 have led many to prefer trickle-up to trickle-down economic policies. However, whatever a reasonable person's preference, the tried-and-tested alternative program to debt and austerity certainly merited discussion and debate by policy makers in the United States after the crisis broke in 2007. Yet that never happened. Republicans and Democrats together repressed the few moves in that direction by various social groups and a handful of dissidents in Congress. Not only was the trickle-up alternative never seriously debated, but any systemic alternative to capitalism—one that might avoid or better manage downturns—was likewise kept off the national agenda, despite the depth and duration of the capitalist crisis and its immense social costs.

2.3 The Bailouts, Monetary Agencies, and Monetary Policies

Classical monetary policy entails lowering interest rates and increasing the money supply to counteract an economic downturn. This task traditionally falls to a nation's central bank. In the United States for the past century, that has meant the Federal Reserve system. Indeed, since 2007, the Federal Reserve has driven interest rates down and kept them down to an unprecedented degree. It has likewise dramatically increased the money supply (commonly described in the financial press as "quantitative easing").

Because of the political conditions I discussed above, when the 2007 crisis hit, politicians remained hesitant about expanding deficits and the debt. The limits they observed meant that fiscal policy could not end or overcome the crisis. As leading Keynesian economists kept lamenting, expansionary deficits were too little and too late. Therefore a disproportionate share of the burden of overcoming the crisis fell to monetary policy and to the Fed. Its chairman, Ben Bernanke, bemoaned that burden repeatedly.

In March 2008, the Fed provided funds to JPMorgan Chase to buy out the investment bank Bear Stearns at a subsidized price. In September 2008, the Fed provided an $85 billion loan to AIG in return for an 80 percent stake in the company. This was crucial to reassure owners of CDS (insurance policies on ABS holdings) and all other participants in credit markets that the debts underlying ABS would be paid. Increasingly, the Federal Reserve moved on multiple fronts to unfreeze the credit markets. It purchased "illiquid," "distressed," and "toxic" securities of all kinds and maturities from banks and other financial enterprises, sometimes on its own and sometimes in buying partnerships with private enterprises. The Fed also provided massive loans to the same sorts of enterprises under the Term Asset-Backed Securities Loan Facility. The Fed poured huge sums into buying debt and mortgage-backed securities from Fannie Mae, Freddie Mac, and Ginnie Mae, the major government supports for the US housing industry, which were eventually taken over by the US government. These and many other programs, both traditional Fed operations and new innovations to unfreeze credit quickly, moved trillions of dollars of bad assets off of private financial enterprises' balance sheets and onto those of the Fed and the US Treasury.

Monetary agencies also insured private debts as well as deposits of various sorts. For example, the Federal Deposit Insurance Corporation (FDIC) administered the Temporary Liquidity Guarantee Program (TLGP), which provided guarantees for both non-interest-bearing transaction accounts at FDIC-covered banks and also for those banks' senior debt. The amounts involved reached into the hundreds of billions.

In short, the United States mobilized many of its financial and monetary agencies to massively socialize its monetary system. Private financial enterprises had ceased to be able to function normally in terms of depositing, borrowing, and lending. Their relationships with one another and with the public—the credit system—had frozen. Consequently, by late 2008, most of the major private financial enterprises were technically as defunct or bankrupt as Lehman Brothers had been when it collapsed.

That freeze threatened to spread quickly via the interdependence among all markets in today's global economy. The US government mobilized its agencies and resources to buy, lend, insure, guarantee, and invest trillions for as many years into the future as necessary to secure two interrelated goals. The first goal was to prevent the freeze from spreading into the nonfinancial aspects of the economy. The second goal was to dissolve the freeze so that credit flows could resume sufficiently to enable the economy to work its way through the crisis, bottom out, and eventually return to economic growth.

The Obama administration provided the vast funds and guarantees necessary to achieve these goals. At the same time, it endlessly repeated the notion that it was "assisting" rather than "replacing" the private banking sector of US capitalism. Together with the banks themselves, the government spread the ideological message that the socialization or nationalization of banking had not happened, that banks unable to function without massive government supports were nonetheless still "private enterprises." The government's supports were always referred to as "temporary," although no one could know how long each of them might be continued or whether and when they might need to be resumed. Even when the US government purchased shares in major US banks and other corporations, they were mostly "nonvoting" shares. The point again was to maintain and underscore the largely fictional "private" nature of these companies that were so utterly dependent on government support to survive.

Among the most remarkable aspects of the rapid and intense socialization of banking and credit in the United States starting in 2008 were its leaders and its taboos. The leaders were most of the CEOs of the nation's largest financial enterprises. After years of speeches celebrating private enterprise as the engine of growth and prosperity and denouncing government as the source of economic inefficiency and waste, those CEOs led the rush to Washington for trillions in assistance. They took what was offered and more. The socialization of US financial enterprises and markets was not the work of social critics, radicals, or Marxists. The finance CEOs managed it to serve their interests. Perhaps now it will be better understood that capitalists rarely oppose government intervention per se—even though they like to say so to stave off unwanted kinds of government intervention. What they want—and what they embrace en masse—is other kinds of government intervention. They want the government to facilitate their profitable activities, clean up the periodic economic messes they make, keep them firmly in charge of finance and credit, and make the general public, rather than the financial industry, pay the huge costs of all that.

The remarkable taboo successfully observed in the US mainstream was that this socialization was not happening, that private financial enterprises remained private and functioning, even when one and often both of these adjectives did not apply. This taboo extended to include public discussions of what should be done in response to the financial dimensions of the crisis—in Congress, the media, and academia—with very few exceptions. Virtually no one reasoned publicly that a private banking and credit system that performed so poorly and with such disastrous economic and social consequences had forfeited the right to continue.

After all, banks and many other financial enterprises are considered "intermediaries." They take deposits, loans, and investments from others and then parcel out those funds to various borrowers for various uses. They are supposed to perform this vital economic function, on which a credit-based economy like ours depends, with expert care, prudence, caution, and ongoing oversight. After all, they are distributing other people's money and funding the activities shaping the economy's trajectory into the future—and hence all of our lives. These private financial enterprises occupy a very consequential place in our society; they have social duties to perform. They can and should be judged accordingly.

Perhaps most importantly, to safeguard the funds of their depositors, lenders, and investors, private financial enterprises are entrusted to choose those to whom they lend with care, exercising what the applicable laws call "due diligence." Banks and other private financial enterprises are supposed to evaluate borrowers' creditworthiness at the time a loan is extended but also throughout its duration. These private financial enterprises—and the larger society they are supposed to serve—need to be assured that the borrower can repay the loan and its interest costs. If private financial enterprises purchase insurance (CDS) on outstanding loans, they need to be sure that the private financial insurers can pay legitimate claims in the event of defaults by borrowers.

In fact, since 2007, the crisis has repeatedly demonstrated that most of the larger private financial enterprises (and many smaller ones as well) performed their obligations disastrously. Their failures to serve society's need for safe and effective financial intermediation led to huge social losses and costs. Yet there was an effective taboo against drawing one obvious inference from those failures. Almost no one in politics, the establishment media, or academia dared to say that such failures of a private finance system raised the question of how a public financial system might function better. There were proposals to allow markets to punish failing banks, to allow the government greater regulatory oversight (as formalized in the later Dodd-Frank legislation), and for greater transparency. But such proposals could not and did not challenge the continuation of financial enterprises as private institutions. It was beyond the pale to suggest the nationalization of banks and other financial enterprises to guarantee the proper performance that private enterprises had failed so spectacularly to achieve, even as the nation subsidized their existence for years with trillions of dollars.

I noted earlier that continued high unemployment and its devastating economic effects provoked discussions of countless stimulus programs, but always while respecting the basic taboo on a federal jobs program. The vast preponderance of political, media, and intellectual discussions swirled around the pros and cons of programs to stimulate or encourage or provide incentives for private employers to hire more people. The fact that from 2009 to 2012, such programs failed to diminish unemployment in any serious way (let alone end it) did not lead to proposals to fashion contemporary equivalents of Roosevelt's federal employment program. Capitalist economies, including that of the United States, have a long history of limiting, regulating, or socializing enterprises and industries whose profit-maximizing strategies risk undermining those of capitalist enterprises collectively. Thus, to take but a few examples, transportation and communication industries have been managed in this way across many societies. In the United States, every one of the fifty states has an insurance commission to monitor and regulate profits of enterprises in that industry—after a long experience of its negative consequences for other capitalist industries and society as a whole generated outcries and alliances strong enough to impose commissions on the insurance industry. Much the same applies to the enterprises in the public utility industries (such as electricity, gas, and water). Monopolies have been repeatedly broken up for similar reasons.

In Europe, several countries have at various times nationalized their banks. That happened historically as a consequence of profound social dissatisfaction with how the profit-driven strategies of private banks contributed to economic crises, with intolerable social costs. In the United States, the Great Depression provoked congressional hearings that revealed extensive conflicts of interest and fraud committed by banks and their investment subsidiaries. The resulting Emergency Banking Relief Act of 1933 (the Glass-Steagall Act) gave the Federal Reserve the power to regulate savings accounts interest rates and also prohibited bank-holding companies from owning other kinds of financial enterprises in order to stop banks from using their depositors' funds for risky investments. Such controls of what private capitalists could charge and do were steps toward—even as they stopped short of—a full nationalization of banking.

The Dodd-Frank Wall Street Reform and Consumer Protection Act of 2010 was the parallel, though much weaker, banking reform legislation for the post-2007 crisis. It similarly flowed from hearings and widespread recognition of the multiple ways in which banking practices had contributed to this major capitalist crisis. Indeed, there were obvious similarities in how private capitalist financial enterprises had contributed to both crises. As many commentators noted, the latest capitalist crisis exploded a mere eight years after Glass-Steagall was finally repealed in 1999. Major US banks had led the way toward that repeal through years of lobbying and public relations campaigns. Immediately after achieving its repeal, those same banks proceeded to commingle depositors' funds and risky ABS and CDS investments in just the ways Glass-Steagall was meant to prevent. Not surprisingly, that speculative commingling once again helped produce a mammoth downturn.

Glass-Steagall had always been an unwanted burden on major US banks. After it passed despite their opposition, banks responded with various strategies to evade its provisions and then to weaken and eventually repeal it. They succeeded in 1999 under President Clinton, a Democrat. Even when 2007 ushered in another major crisis and overwhelming evidence of the complicity of banks in producing it, the major banks were successful in preventing the re-enactment of Glass-Steagall provisions in new laws. Large banks and major corporations had generally changed political conditions in their favor. They had learned how to devote more resources in better ways to influence legislative outcomes.

At the height of the post-2007 crisis, major banks demanded and received massive government help on the basis of a threat. They were, they insisted, "too big to fail." The idea seemed to be that letting them collapse or default would have such devastating consequences for the larger economy that the government had to help them "in the national interest." The fallout from the collapse of the Lehman Brothers investment bank was used as the perfect example of why such a "colossal mistake" could not be replicated. They used such arguments in public and congressional debates, eventually garnering trillions of dollars in government support.

However, the banks' arguments had two logical implications that had to be blocked from public discussion, let alone action. More taboos were thereby revealed. The first implication was that such large enterprises should be broken up into smaller enterprises so that the failure of any one would not effectively blackmail the government into costly support. So effectively were the few public statements in that direction ignored and repressed that nothing much was said—and certainly nothing was done—about the fact that many of the major US banks were significantly larger in 2012 than they had been in 2007. If there was a "moral hazard" that bailing out big banks during and after 2008 might weaken their resolve to avoid excess risk thereafter, then allowing big banks to become bigger accelerated the moral hazard involved.

The second implication that had to be repressed was this: if big banks and other financial enterprises were too big to fail, then perhaps the solution was to nationalize them. Making their assets and liabilities fully transparent and publicly available would minimize the chance of behaviors that placed society at risk. Officials of government banking agencies would be subject to political scrutiny and to elections, thereby making them more accountable. The dependence of enterprises and the public on electricity, water, postal service, the broadcast spectrum, and other such services has led governments in many countries to either regulate or nationalize the private enterprises producing those services. When regulation proves inadequate or insufficient, nationalization is often a logical next step. However, neoliberal ideology effectively enforced a taboo against recognizing this implication of the "too big to fail" arguments.

In the end, the last century of capitalism teaches a profound truth by means of repeated, specific lessons regarding government economic interventions that regulate, limit, or constrain capitalists' goals. Such economic interventions are resisted by major capitalist enterprises. If they pass into law, corporations use their expanding resources (rising net incomes) to evade, weaken, and eliminate those restrictions, as we saw with the successful campaign to repeal Glass-Steagall. There are many other examples in the United States and in other countries. In European countries where banks, public utilities, and transportation enterprises were nationalized, capitalists responded likewise and have often succeeded in reprivatizing them.

Simply put, so long as a major economic sector consists of large private capitalist enterprises accumulating rising net incomes, they can and will devote energy and resources to removing government interventions they do not want. Government economic interventions that constrain large capitalist enterprises in the pursuit of the rising profits, market shares, and growth rates they seek are therefore always fundamentally insecure. This applies to government regulation as well as partial or selective nationalizations of private capitalist enterprises. A good metaphor for the historical lesson here is this: in a war that ends with the victor imposing heavy, enduring burdens on the loser, the victor must also disarm the loser. Otherwise, the loser will be tempted to use the arms it has retained to relieve those burdens.

In the political wars that imposed regulations and partial, selective nationalizations on major capitalist enterprises, those corporate enterprises retained capitalist structures. Their small collectives of major shareholders and boards of directors provided them with the incentives and resources to overturn the regulations and nationalizations. In most modern capitalist economies, the Great Depression of the 1930s produced government regulations and nationalizations because of pressure from working-class organizations (labor unions and left political parties). In each case, after 1945, the larger capitalist enterprises in those countries used their resources to evade, weaken, and eliminate the restrictions. The timing and extent of their successes has varied with the specific historical conditions and balance of class forces in each country.

As I will show in detail in the second part of this book, the historical lesson about the reversibility of nationalization and regulation of capitalist enterprises applies also to the state-socialist societies in the USSR, elsewhere in Eastern Europe, and beyond. In short, it applies to general and widespread, as well as partial and selective, nationalizations. Where state officials have replaced boards of directors elected by major shareholders—and thus where workers continue to produce surpluses and profits for others—such state officials will also face incentives and deploy resources to deregulate and denationalize their enterprises as conditions permit.

3 Crises, Forms of Capitalism, and Beyond

Across its history, the basic elements of capitalism have changed little, while other aspects of it have changed a great deal. One aspect that has remained nearly constant is the class structure of production. By that I mean the internal organization of enterprises. Under capitalism, a mass of workers produce by their labor more than they get back as wages and salaries. In the language of economics, the value added by workers in production exceeds the value paid to those workers for the work they do. The difference between the value added by workers and the value paid to workers is what Karl Marx called surplus.

3.1 Capitalism

In capitalist enterprises, the producers of surplus are different people than the appropriators of that surplus. The employer versus employee differential is a constant feature, whether it is a small

79

individual capitalist with a few worker-employees or a huge modern mega-corporation with a board of directors that appropriates the surplus produced by tens or hundreds of thousands of employees. The capitalists—those who appropriate the surplus in each enterprise—distribute the surplus as payments mostly to other people whose activities help to reproduce that capitalist enterprise (interest to creditors, salaries and budgets to the enterprise's managers, taxes to the state, dividends to shareholders, and so on).

One aspect of capitalist economies that has periodically changed is the relationship among the state, private citizens, and capitalist enterprises. In what can be called "private capitalism," the employers are private citizens who hold no position within the state apparatus and operate with relatively minimal interventions by the state. In what we can call "state capitalism," the employers are officials within the state apparatus. Between private and state capitalism, we have a range of intermediary situations where state officials operate all sorts of regulations and interventions shaping and influencing private capitalists, but do not become capitalist employers themselves. We might call that state-regulated private capitalism to distinguish it from both private and state forms of capitalism.

The term capitalism applies to all three possible situations because the internal organization of productive enterprises is the same in each of them: production is organized such that hired workers produce surpluses appropriated and distributed by people other than themselves, employers who are either private or state capitalists. Modern societies' economic, political, and cultural relationships, their dynamics, tensions, and conflicts, are all shaped in part by that particular capitalist way of organizing the production of commodities.*

---

* If and when other, noncapitalist ways of organization production exist, they shape the larger society in other ways. For example, collective or communist enterprises

The histories of societies in which capitalism is the prevailing organization of production have everywhere been punctuated by periodic, recurring crises. These have beset both more- and less-regulated private capitalism and also state capitalism. Such crises have provoked oscillations within national capitalisms among their private and state forms. So, for example, when private capitalisms encounter their recurring downturns, they have often turned toward more state regulation to offset, moderate, or reverse those downturns. Moderate and short downturns usually generate relatively limited increases in state regulations, whereas worse downturns tend to provoke more and deeper state regulation. The Great Depression of the 1930s illustrated both degrees of regulation as it cycled through its multiple downturns. Sometimes the reaction to and critique of private capitalism, in more severe and longer-lasting economic downturns, produce a transition beyond regulated private capitalism to a form of state capitalism. That happened in Russia after 1917 and in several other countries after the Great Depression and since.

3.2 State Capitalism

In state capitalism, the employers are state officials who have replaced the former private capitalists. In the new Soviet Union, for

---

(where the producers and appropriators of the surplus are the same people) shape society and history differently. The same applies to a slave organization of production (where masters appropriate the entire output of slaves) or a self-employed organization (where an individual worker appropriates her or his own surplus) and so on. In typical societies where multiple, different organizations of production coexist, the society and its history reflect influences flowing from them all—and tensions and conflicts among them as well. For a full discussion of these different organizations (or "class structures") of production—with special emphasis on the capitalist and the communist—see Stephen Resnick and Richard Wolff, *Class Theory and History: Capitalism, Communism and the USSR* (New York and London: Routledge, 2002). There we explain how and why the term socialism came to be redefined as state capitalism.

example, immediately after the 1917 revolution, the government closed the stock market, largely dispossessed private shareholders of their industrial enterprises, and nationalized those enterprises. There were some temporary and limited experiments with noncapitalist organizations of production in the postrevolutionary USSR. In those experiments, workers were, collectively, both the producers and the appropriators of surpluses. However, despite the socialist commitments of the leaders and activists who led the revolution, those experiments were abandoned under multiple pressures (discussed in detail in my book written with Stephen Resnick, *Class Theory and History*). Soviet socialism—and increasingly socialism in general—came to be redefined in terms of what actually existed inside Soviet industrial enterprises. There, hired workers produced surpluses that were appropriated and distributed by others: the council of ministers, state officials who functioned as employers. Thus Soviet industry was actually an example of state capitalism in its class structure. However, by describing itself increasingly as socialist, it prompted the redefinition of socialism to mean state capitalism.

To complicate matters, in the 1930s there were also some more radical voices calling for transitions to "socialism" who did not thereby mean state capitalism. Instead they wanted to reorganize the production system so that workers themselves appropriated and distributed the surpluses they produced. Socialism increasingly meant different things to different people. However, what prevailed in the "actually existing socialist societies" that developed after 1917 were state-capitalist class structures of production. State capitalism provoked crises much as private capitalism did. The shape and management of the crises differed within the two kinds of capitalism, just as they differed between more- and less-regulated private capitalism. What was similar across the crises in all sorts of capitalism was the typical rise of demands to overcome a crisis in any one kind of capitalism by transitioning to another kind. In the Great Depression of the 1930s, for example, demands arose for both a transition from private to regulated private capitalism and a transition from private to state capitalism (referred to as "socialism"). Sometimes the proponents of these different anti-crisis programs worked together as allies against the conservative advocates of continued private capitalism. At other times, they split because of their different notions of how best to overcome capitalism's crisis. Likewise, when a major crisis overtook the Soviet Union in the 1980s, its critical movements eventually became divided chiefly between those who wanted to move toward regulated private capitalism and those who wanted to move to a relatively unregulated private capitalism. They also sometimes worked together and sometimes split in their opposition to conservative movements seeking to retain state capitalism.

The capitalist crisis since 2007 has generated demands for a transition to a more regulated private capitalism and also for a transition to state capitalism. Interestingly, such demands have come from both capitalists and workers, in diverse combinations. Thus, many recent critics of the relatively less-regulated (neoliberal) private capitalism that has prevailed in the United States since the 1970s have demanded a sharply increased regulatory role for the government. So, too, have segments of the employer class, who fear the possible political and social consequences of maintaining neoliberal capitalism. Likewise, the revival of interest in socialism as an alternative to capitalism has produced advocates of state capitalism—understood as "socialism"—as the necessary solution for a crisis-ridden private capitalism. Segments of the employer class have reached similar conclusions as they compared the crippling effects of the post-2007 crisis on private capitalism (both more and less regulated) and the much better performance of, for example, state capitalism in China.

Once again, in the current aftermath of the latest major capitalist crisis, we confront a simple truth. In every previous crisis, various policy advocates promised that their policies would not only lead the way out of crisis, but also prevent future crises from crippling capitalist economies. None of those policies, when applied, ever achieved that second objective. Future crises were never yet prevented, as the historical record attests.

So stunning and relentless a record of failures to prevent crises provides yet another reason to go beyond the ineffective oscillation among various forms of capitalism. Overcoming the crises that are endemic to capitalism requires changing more than the form of capitalism. It requires changing the internal organization of capitalist production itself. In precisely this sense, a solution to capitalism's oscillations between private and state forms that rejects both could redefine socialism (and breathe contemporary urgency into it) by returning to an earlier and more radically anticapitalist definition of the term.

◆ ◆ ◆

The central thesis of this book is that moving beyond the internal organization of capitalist enterprises toward a specific, democratic alternative organization of production is the way forward now. Not only does a transition to worker-directed enterprises offer better prospects for preventing future crises, it also entails solutions for a host of related problems that have long defined capitalist societies. In the remainder of this book, I make the case for that transition.

Part II:

What Is to Be Done?

In part I of this book, I analyzed the post-2007 crisis of capitalism in the context of the recurring crises that have always plagued capitalism. I argued that overcoming crisis requires something more than further oscillations between its private and state forms. It requires a basic change in the internal organization of productive enterprises. In chapter 4, I argue for the need to move beyond private capitalism. In chapter 5, I will make parallel arguments about why we also need to move beyond state capitalism.

4 The Major Problems of Private Capitalisms

The functioning of capitalist economies depends crucially on the decisions made by a relatively small number of capitalists. In the typical larger corporations that prevail in the United States and many other capitalist economies, boards of directors selected by the enterprise's major shareholders are the decision makers. Usually composed of nine to twenty individuals, these boards are very small collectives of capitalists. They make the basic decisions of what to produce (which goods and services), how to produce (what technologies and inputs to utilize), and where to produce (what geographic locations to occupy for producing and distributing their outputs). These decisions are part of what directing the enterprise means.

The capitalists also gather into their hands the surpluses produced by the capitalist enterprises they direct. Those surpluses are the differences in each enterprise between the value added by workers and the value of the wages and salaries paid to them. Capitalists gather the surpluses because the laws, traditions, and ideologies governing capitalism decree that the total output produced by workers is immediately and automatically the property of their employers. At the end of each working day, the workers lay down their tools and equipment and leave the site of production. They also leave behind whatever they produced, because the production of that output was simultaneously its appropriation by the employers.

When the employers sell the output, they realize revenues. They usually use one part of those revenues to pay the employed workers who made the output. They spend another part of those revenues to replenish the tools, equipment, and raw materials used up in production. The remaining part of the revenues is the surplus, roughly the difference between the enterprise's revenues and the basic costs of producing whatever the enterprise sells.

4.1 Distributing the Surplus

The capitalists must distribute the surplus among a variety of people and enterprises that perform functions considered necessary to keep those capitalists in business. For example, part of the surplus must be distributed to managers who work in the enterprise's sales department, whose task is to sell whatever the enterprise produces. Sales managers need salaries and budgets (for staff, equipment, and so on) to make sure the enterprise's outputs are sold. But the managers and their staff are not among the workers who make whatever the enterprise sells. The work of managers and their staff is not productive of output in that sense, but it is surely crucial to the success and viability of the capitalist enterprise. Only if the enterprise's outputs are sold will its capitalists obtain the revenues needed to keep the capitalist enterprise in business (for example, to pay workers their cash wages and to buy the tools and equipment needed to replace those that wear out). Capitalists usually pay for their sales departments by distributing a portion of the surpluses they appropriate from the output-producing workers. The same sort of analysis applies to lawyers, security guards, creditors, and others who provide non-output-producing activities that capitalists require.

The capitalists also distribute portions of the surplus to the government as taxes and fees to secure crucial public services on which the enterprise's survival depends, such as public education, police, road maintenance, and so on. Capitalist corporations typically distribute another portion of the surplus to shareholders as dividends to secure their investments and confidence in the enterprise. Finally, capitalists distribute a portion of the surplus to themselves to pay for expanding the enterprise as a competitive strategy to stay in business. In the language of business, the portions of the surplus that capitalists pay out in dividends and use for expansion are called "profits."

Directing a capitalist enterprise includes the processes of appropriating and distributing the surplus generated within it. Those processes are as basic to directing a capitalist enterprise as are making and enforcing the decisions about what, how, and where to produce. In capitalist economies, the people who direct enterprises—who appropriate and distribute surpluses and who decide what, where, and how to produce—are capitalists. Moreover, they are distinguished from workers, those hired by capitalists, by the fact that workers are excluded from directing capitalist enterprises. Thus the object and focus of this book—workers' self-directed enterprises—represents an economic evolution beyond and different from capitalism.

How capitalists direct enterprises plays a major role in shaping capitalist societies. For example, to whom and for what purposes capitalists distribute the surplus influences the culture and politics, as well as the economics, of capitalist societies. If capitalists are concerned about matters of crime and security, they can and will distribute large portions of the surplus to preventing crime, prosecuting those they deem criminals, and obtaining security. That will create a demand for and call forth a supply of workers to learn and perform those tasks. Capitalists' distributions of surpluses to those ends will influence the entire society's perceptions and conceptions of criminal dangers.

To take another example, if capitalists believe that top managerial executives such as CEOs play crucial roles in generating enterprise profits and growth, they can allocate huge portions of the surplus to them as salaries, bonuses, stock options, and so on. This will likely result in widening income inequality, especially if combined with decisions to relocate production from higher to lower wage locations, to replace workers with machines, and so on. Stagnant or falling wage levels, combined with growing allocations of surpluses to top managers' fast-rising pay packages, can generate a political and cultural polarization based on growing income and wealth inequality.

Capitalists who are concerned about securing sufficient sales of their enterprise's outputs may allocate large portions of their surplus to sales efforts, advertising, and so on, thereby shaping, enlarging, redirecting, or otherwise changing the mechanisms of advertising, the mass media, and cultural institutions.

4.2 Private Capitalism and Democracy

The problems of capitalism flow in part from who directs productive enterprises and how they direct them. In capitalism, the directors are the capitalists; workers are excluded from direction.

Driven by competition and other aspects of the system, capitalists direct the what, how, and where of production and the distribution of the surpluses they appropriate in their enterprises in very particular ways. Capitalists define goals such as maximizing profits and achieving high rates of growth or larger market shares, and then direct their enterprises accordingly. Capitalists routinely pursue those goals, often at the expense of their workers. For example, they fire workers and replace them with machines, or they impose a technology that exposes workers to health and environmental risks but increases profits, or they relocate production out of the country to exploit cheaper labor. However, if enterprises were organized differently—if workers collectively directed enterprises (and thus excluded capitalists)—the problems of enterprises would be solved in different ways, with different social consequences. I will develop this key point in detail in part III of this book.

In societies where the private capitalist organization of production prevails, the workers—the vast majority of the people—must live with the results of capitalists' decisions in directing enterprises. However, they are allowed no general participation in those decisions. Sometimes, workers, alone or allied with others, can influence capitalists' allocations of an enterprise's surplus. If, for example, workers threaten job actions while consumers threaten to boycott an enterprise's products, their alliance might achieve changed surplus allocations to meet their respective demands. These might include, for example, job-site daycare facilities for workers' children, medical insurance for workers and their families, and even pay supplements beyond basic wages. Capitalists recognize, in such cases, that the reproduction of their enterprises requires allocating some surplus to such usages.

Generally, the appropriation and distribution of enterprise surpluses is the exclusive right and responsibility of the capitalists, not the workers. Thus the problems of modern capitalism—for example, environmental degradation, extremely unequal distributions of income and wealth, and recurring, socially costly business cycles—result in significant ways from how capitalists direct their enterprises. Derivative problems—for example, the undermining of democracy as corporations and the rich protect their disproportionate wealth and power by corrupting politics—also result, to a significant degree, from how capitalists direct their enterprises.

Modern markets confront each capitalist enterprise with the competitive threat that another enterprise will be able to offer an alternative product of higher quality, lower price, or both. The uncertainties of changing tastes and preferences, changing interest rates for loans, changing prices for necessary inputs, and so on confront enterprises with a vast array of threats to their survival. Political shifts in the larger society mean that the taxes they have to pay, regulations they have to endure, and subsidies they may lose can also threaten their survival.

The typical capitalist enterprise's response is to seek more profits, increase the size of the company, or gain a bigger share of the market. Different enterprises stress one or another of these goals, depending on which is more important or available for its survival. Achieving these goals strengthens the capacity of the enterprise to prevent or lessen or absorb the endless array of threats it faces. Likewise, achieving these goals improves the enterprise's capacity to take advantage of any opportunity that arises. Thus, for example, greater profits enable an enterprise to make the investments needed to tap a new market; faster growth attracts capital and good press reports; and a larger market share can secure lower prices for larger quantities of purchased inputs.

In short, what capitalists do is governed by the system that unites the enterprises directed by capitalists, the markets in which they buy and sell, and the larger society and government for which they provide the bulk of goods and services. Capitalists respond to the signals they receive from the markets, the media, the government, and so on. The goals they pursue—profits, growth, and market share—are their rational responses to those signals. That pursuit is how the capitalist system defines their tasks or jobs. How well capitalists achieve these goals plays a major role in determining their remuneration, their social prestige, and their self-esteem.

Indeed, some capitalists come to internalize the system's rules and imperatives. They define themselves and mold their personalities in conformity with the behaviors imposed on them as capitalists. So it may seem and be said—even by capitalists themselves—that they are greedy or have other character flaws. However, when capitalists, for example, try to squeeze more work out of employees while trying to pay them less, replace workers with machines, relocate production to low-wage areas, risk their workers' health with cheap but toxic inputs, and so on—those are behaviors prompted in them by the realities of the system within which they work and for which they are rewarded and praised. Many capitalists do these things without being greedy or evil. When capitalists do display greed or other character flaws, those flaws are less causes than results of a system that requires certain actions by capitalists who want to survive and prosper.

The many different problems and failures of the capitalist system we have been discussing pertain to private capitalisms, whether they are more or less regulated. These problems and failures follow in large part from the internal organization of capitalist enterprises. Their directors often respond to the threats and opportunities facing the enterprise in ways that damage the interests of their workers, the workers' families, and the larger communities. That is how the system works and generates its particular and often serious economic problems.

What happens if we shift our focus from economics to politics? Politics in the United States has become utterly dependent on and corrupted by financial contributions to candidates, political parties, lobbyists, think tanks, and special committees, recently further enabled by the Citizens United Supreme Court decision. The disparity of interests between capitalists and workers and the disparity of the concentrated resources they can and do devote to supporting their favored positions, politicians, and parties undermine a democratic politics.

In fact, we must question the very possibility of genuine democracy in a society in which capitalism is the basic economic system. A functioning democracy would require that all people be provided with the time, information, counsel, and other supports needed to participate effectively in decision-making in the workplace and at the local, regional, and national levels of their residential communities. The economic realities of capitalism preclude that for the overwhelming majority of workers, in stark contrast to corporate directors, top managers, their professional staff, and all those with significant incomes from property (above all, their property in shares of capitalist enterprises). Such persons also have concentrated wealth in the forms of their enterprises' surpluses and/or their personal property that they can donate to their preferred representatives among the society's major institutions, parties, and candidates. The political leadership created through such networks in turn advances these groups' interests in a capitalist system that rewards them richly. Only a highly mobilized and coordinated organization of the workers could hope to secure the financial resources that might begin seriously to contest the political power of capitalists'. money by combining very small contributions from a very large number of donors. This possibility has sufficiently concerned capitalist interests that they have devoted enormous resources to sustaining opposition to workers' organizations. That opposition helped to produce the last fifty years' decline in US labor union membership as a percentage of workers and of political parties seeking to represent workers' interests against those of capitalists.

It is important to note that combinations and coalitions of corporate directors, top managers, large shareholders, and their various professional staffs have often used their financial resources in struggles among themselves. These groups have and pursue some conflicting interests. However, their struggles do not blind them to common interests in securing the political conditions of the capitalist economic system. Thus they worked together to secure the massive US government intervention to overcome the capitalist crisis that hit in 2007, even though the bailouts went more to some firms and industries than to others. Similarly, they nearly all endorsed the refusal of the Bush and Obama administrations to undertake a federal hiring program to slash unemployment, even though firms and industries would be differently affected by such a program.

In the decades since the 1970s, stagnant real wages, rising hours of paid labor performed per person and per household, and rising levels of household debt all combined to leave working families with less time and energy to devote to politics—or indeed to social activities and organizations in general.* Working-class participation in politics, already limited before the 1970s, shrank very significantly during the neoliberal period. At the same time, the soaring profits of US business and personal wealth of the richest Americans increasingly

---

* See the ample documentation of this point in Robert D. Putnam, *Bowling Alone: the Collapse and Revival of American Community* (New York: Simon and Schuster, 2000).

poured into US politics. In the first place, they had quickly growing resources that allowed them to influence politics to a greater extent than ever before. In the second place, they had greater incentives to do so than ever before. The inequalities of individual wealth and income in the United States were growing. The profitability of business, and especially of the largest corporations, was likewise growing. This posed a challenge. Rising economic inequalities are always issues of concern to those at the top because of the risks of envy, resentment, and opposition. There is always the possibility that the economically disadvantaged will seek to use political means to recoup their losses in the economy. The 99 percent might turn to politics to negate the economic gains of the 1 percent. Thus it became—and remains—more important than ever for the 1 percent to use their money to shape and control politics.

The last three decades of US politics did not see a change of political opinion from more left to more right. Rather, what happened was a relative withdrawal from politics of those social groups that favored social-welfare and income-redistribution policies (the New Deal "legacy") and a relative increase in the participation of business and the rich, who used their money to shift the tone and content of US politics.

The result of this political shift has compounded the social costs and negative impacts of the economic crisis since 2007. Our dysfunctional economic system has suffered the added burden of a dysfunctional political system. Political parties and politicians stumble over one another in pandering to corporations and the rich. Thus the TARP program of 2008 provided money to bail out banks and other corporations while also claiming to help the millions facing foreclosure. While the bailouts were accomplished, foreclosure assistance was trivial and far below even what little had been promised. If this was trickle-down economics, workers saw only a very slight trickle. Bush and then Obama have insisted on limiting government programs to reduce unemployment to those that "provide incentives and encouragement to the private sector" to hire more people. The political establishments in both parties refuse to discuss federal programs to hire the millions of workers who are unemployed. Instead, the crisis since 2007 has prompted all levels of government to cut many programs and payrolls, imposing "austerity" budgets just when the mass of people need exactly the opposite. A virtual political taboo precludes public discussion of how the costs for more government spending and larger government payrolls could be defrayed by taxing corporations and the rich. That would be an anti-crisis "trickle-up" government economic policy that does not entail deficits or raise the national debt.

What prevents another New Deal–type trickle-up economic policy from being adopted now is a political system compromised by its dependence on money drawn predominantly from certain social groups. Not surprisingly, those groups insist on trickle-down economics. The government helps them first, foremost, and overwhelmingly. The rest of the economy and society then wait to see what, if anything, actually trickles down.

Meanwhile, the total losses for the US economy for the years since 2007 far exceed what could have been spent to keep the economy going. Since 2007, many millions of newly unemployed and around 20 percent of our productive capacity have been sitting idle. Those people want to work; our economy wants and needs the wealth they could create to solve many of our nation's and the world's problems. However, our private capitalist economic system cannot bring together the unemployed with the idle tools, equipment, and raw materials to produce that wealth. And a dysfunctional political system does nothing about that.

The development of US capitalism, especially since the 1970s, has produced extreme economic inequality, the second major crisis in the last seventy-five years, and a political system in which money trumps democracy. To change this requires a cure for capitalism that targets both its economic and political problems directly and effectively. In part III of this book, I sketch the main features of such a cure.

5 The Major Problems of State Capitalism

Since its inception, capitalism has had both celebrants and critics. Criticisms of capitalism, while diverse, have largely coalesced into a major global tradition of anticapitalist theories and practices that have mostly taken the names "socialism" or "communism" over the last 150 years. While there have been important differences among and between socialist and communist theories and practices, they are secondary to the points and purposes of this chapter. I will therefore refer generally to socialism and take it to include its varieties and communism, unless otherwise indicated.

Socialist theory has historically included both critiques of capitalism and constructions of hypothetical alternative economic and social systems. As socialist ideas spread and came to be held by large groups of people, they took the form of statements, platforms, and programs advocated by social movements, organizations such as labor unions, and political parties. People and organizations committed to socialism were sometimes able to construct small socialist communities within larger nonsocialist societies. These were religious or secular, rural or urban, market- or non-market oriented, short-lived or longer lasting, and diverse in other ways. In the latter half of the nineteenth century in Europe, socialist movements became strong enough to take power in major cities and even whole nations via general strikes, insurrections, revolutions, or parliamentary elections. The Paris Commune of 1870–71 marks one major milestone of socialist development; the Russian Revolution of 1917 marks another. There have been many other milestones over the last century.

As socialism spread after the 1860s—especially via the powerfully influential writings of Karl Marx and Friedrich Engels—it entered into the debates and social movements of many different countries at quite different levels of economic development and with quite different mixtures of capitalist and noncapitalist economic systems. These countries also had very different political traditions and cultures. Correspondingly different understandings of socialism and interpretations of Marx's and Engels's works contributed to a rich and diverse tradition. However, for many reasons, two key differences became almost universally accepted as defining and differentiating capitalism and socialism. Those key differences then shaped the intellectual struggles between devotees of the two systems, the political struggles between social movements and parties committed to different systems, and the changes brought about by successful revolutions.

5.1 Key Differences between Capitalism and Socialism

The first key difference between capitalism and socialism deals with who owns the means of production: land, machines, factories, offices, and so on. Capitalism is the system in which private property predominates. The means of production are privately owned and are contributed to production only if in return the private owners obtain a share of the production's output (the surplus or profit). In contrast, socialism is defined as a system in which productive property is socialized—becoming the property of the people as a whole—and is then administered by the state for the people as a whole (not for the surplus or profit of private owners).

A second key difference between the two systems lies in how they distribute productive resources (means of production) and outputs among enterprises and citizens. Capitalism is a market system. In capitalist economic systems, resources and outputs are distributed by means of market exchanges, in which their private owners bargain with one another to reach mutually acceptable price ratios for what they exchange. In contrast, socialism is a system that distributes resources and outputs by means of national planning. Rather than allow market exchanges to determine who pays how much to get what, state officials plan production inside state enterprises as well as how resources and outputs are distributed among enterprises and to the consuming public.

Private property and markets are the key economic institutions defining capitalism, whereas state property and planning define the socialist alternative. While those who favored capitalism disagreed about almost everything for much of the last century with those who favored socialism, both sides largely agreed on this definition of the key difference between the two economic systems. Their major debates and conflicts pitted private against socialized property and markets against planning. To this day, these remain the key definitional differences between the two systems for many people.

5.2 Twentieth-Century Socialisms

Over the last 150 years, the problems besetting capitalism—especially periodic crises—have provoked socialist movements, electoral campaigns, and sometimes revolutions. Because socialism has become the major alternative to capitalism in most people's minds, problems in capitalism have almost always provoked interest in socialism as a possible solution. When socialist movements have come to power in capitalist economies, they tend to take steps toward more socialized and less private ownership of means of production and toward more state planning and a reduced role for markets. How fast and how far socialist regimes move away from capitalism and toward socialism, as they defined it, has always depended on the specific economic, political, and cultural conditions in which the socialists come to power.

Thus, for example, when Italy's Communist Party won elections to run several large northern Italian cities during the decades after World War II, it accepted limits on how fast and how far those cities could move toward socialism within a country in which capitalism, not socialism, prevailed. Likewise, when the Socialist Party under François Mitterand won power in France in the 1980s, it only socialized some private capitalist industries, not all, and extended planning to only some parts of the economy. By contrast, in Cuba, the government of Fidel Castro went considerably further toward socialized property and planning than either of these examples. Their different social histories and conditions shaped what their leaders wanted and believed possible as well as the obstacles they faced.

Starting in 1917, first Russia and then a number of other countries, large and small, undertook transitions from capitalist to socialist economic systems (as those terms were popularly understood).

After 1945, the Cold War positioned the two kinds of countries as enemies, with the United States as the leading capitalist country and the Soviet Union as the leading socialist country. They succeeded in avoiding a hot war, but came close on some occasions and also engaged in major conflicts through surrogates in places such as Vietnam, El Salvador, and Chile. Then in the late 1980s, the major socialist countries, particularly the USSR, the People's Republic of China, and their allies, had major crises. In many of them, popular dissatisfaction with socialism prompted movements to return to capitalism. Once in power, those movements proceeded to privatize the means of production, expand the role of markets, and diminish the scope of government economic planning. Once again, this shared view of what differentiated capitalism from socialism shaped the transitions between them.

The history of Russia in the twentieth century included a transition from capitalism to socialism at the beginning and the reverse at the end. More or less similar oscillations from capitalism to socialism and back to capitalism happened in most of the other countries that turned toward socialism in the twentieth century. The return of socialist economic systems to capitalist ones shocked a number of socialist theorists and led them to re-examine their theories. Most socialists had believed that socialism was a higher stage of human development and would not be reversible because people would defend it against the alternative of capitalism. Clearly that belief was mistaken.

5.3 Socialism and Surplus Analysis

In the decades after the 1970s, more and more socialist theorists began to question some of the basic assumptions and arguments of the socialist tradition. Many went back to the greatest socialist theorists—above all to the analytical framework of Marx—and there found new explanations for the collapses and changes of socialist systems during and after the 1980s. A new way of thinking about capitalism and socialism emerged during this period of critical reconsideration of the socialist tradition. It not only provided an explanation for the reverses of socialism, but also opened up a whole new way of understanding certain shared problems of capitalism and socialism—and pointed a way forward to overcome or cure those problems. This book is written from the standpoint of this new way of thinking, which is called "surplus analysis."

From the standpoint of surplus analysis, what defines an economic system—for example, capitalism—is not primarily how productive resources are owned nor how resources and products are distributed. Rather, the key definitional dimension is the organization of production. More precisely, the definitional priority concerns how the production and distribution of the surplus are organized.

Marx is the source of the basic analysis of capitalism in terms of the production and distribution of the surplus.[*] Some major Marxian writers have since further developed that surplus analysis. However, Marx's surplus analysis as a basis for differentiating capitalism and socialism never acquired the centrality that property ownership (private versus public) and resource and product distribution (market versus planning) did in the nearly universally shared definition/differentiation of both systems. Here I propose to enrich and thereby transform that definition/differentiation by adding the organization of the surplus to the analysis. Moreover,

---

[*] Wolff and Resnick, *Contending Economic Theories*. See also *Knowledge and Class* by the same authors.

because the surplus analysis has been so long marginalized or ignored in discussions of capitalism and socialism, I foreground and concentrate on it here.

In capitalism, as I have noted, productive workers add more value to the commodities produced in and sold by the enterprise than the value of their wages paid by the capitalist who hired them. That additional value or surplus is appropriated by the capitalists. They distribute portions of that surplus to a variety of others (and to themselves) to support activities they believe are needed to keep the capitalist enterprise in business. This particular way of organizing the production and distribution of the surplus is capitalism.

What, then, is socialism? If socialism is to be a distinct economic system, then it must clearly differentiate itself from capitalism in terms of how surplus is produced and distributed. Marx's critique of capitalism offers a clue as to the defining characteristic of socialism in his suggestive references to "associated workers" and other images of workers having replaced capitalists as directors of productive enterprises. The alternative economic system that begins to emerge in Marx's writings differs from capitalism in how it organizes the production and distribution of the surplus. Specifically, in a socialist economy, workers—who produce the surplus—themselves appropriate and distribute the surplus. Note that it is precisely the workers—and not a separate, small group of persons, as in capitalism—who play the key roles of appropriating and distributing the surpluses they generate in production. The producers and appropriators of the surplus are then identical: the same group, collective, or community of persons. In such a surplus-focused analysis, socialism and communism are differentiated from capitalism in terms of being nonexploitative, since the producers of surpluses also appropriate and distribute them. Marx saw the presence of such communisms in the past (conceptualized as his "primitive communism") and also envisioned a modern version of them in a postcapitalist future.*

But here we face a dilemma. Most of the anticapitalist movements that called themselves "socialist" in the last century did not prioritize, explicitly include, or—if they came to power—institute an economic system in which the production and distribution of surplus were carried out by those who produced it. That is also true of those that called themselves "communist." Instead, these terms and the differences between them were defined in classic terms of private versus state ownership of the means of production and of market versus planning mechanisms of distribution of resources and products.

Communism came to mean—especially once the Soviet Union was established in 1917—an economic system in which state ownership replaced private ownership quite extensively, especially in industry, and in which planning dominated or even displaced markets as means of distributing resources and products. In contrast, socialism came to mean an economic system in which state ownership went further than was typical of private capitalism (but not as far as in communism) and planning was more economically significant than in private capitalism (but did not displace markets to the extent typical of communism). Thus, for example, most countries in northern Europe have for decades been considered more or less "socialist," although definitely not communist, whereas the Soviet Union, China, and Cuba, for example, have been considered communist. Matters were made murkier because some countries referred to

---

* See Eric Hobsbawm, *Pre-capitalist Economic Formations* (New York: International Publishers, 1971). See also Resnick and Wolff, *Class Theory and History*.

themselves as "socialist" systems aiming to make an eventual transition to communism. The leadership in such countries by a "Communist Party" thus referred to the ultimate goal, not to the current realities of their economic systems, in the sense of positioning workers as appropriators and distributors of the surpluses they produced in workers' self-directed enterprises.

The fundamental point to stress here is that, with a few limited and temporary exceptions, when socialists and communists came to power and instituted new economic systems, they did not prioritize or include workers' self-directed enterprises as basic features of their economies. Neither socialism nor communism advocated or put in place the noncapitalist economic system I have described in this book as workers' self-directed enterprises. However much they wanted to or thought they had, they did not take society beyond capitalism to an alternative system. What they had achieved—partially in the case of socialists and more extensively in the case of communists—were changes in the form of capitalism.

Socialists and communists moved from private to state forms of capitalism. Socialists moved relatively moderately, while communists moved less moderately. Both advocated and instituted a much larger role for the government in the economy. Socialists wanted the state to regulate, control, and partially socialize private capitalist enterprises. Communists wanted the state to more extensively and intensively regulate and monitor, but also to more thoroughly socialize, the means of production.

However, there were always dissenting socialists and Marxists who critically evaluated state capitalisms from a socialist perspective. Other socialists and Marxists developed this space in multiple ways. Some criticized USSR-type socialisms on the grounds of their inadequate or absent democratic institutions; they contrasted top-down with bottom-up constructions of socialist systems. Many questioned the durability or even the possibility of genuine socialism if unaccompanied by genuine democracy. My argument shares the critique of top-down organizations of socialism. However, it differs from others in locating the problem more specifically in the production and distribution of the surpluses. By positioning workers within each productive enterprise as themselves the appropriators and distributors of that enterprise's surpluses, the economic system is itself democratized. Then it can support and facilitate a democratic polity. When workers directly receive and distribute the surpluses they produce, democracy is finally grounded economically. Part III develops this argument much further.

In sum, what socialists and communists have sought were different degrees of state capitalism.* The Soviet leader Lenin had the courage and clarity to use the term "state capitalism" to describe what he and the other Bolsheviks had achieved by the early 1920s in the Soviet Union. He saw it as a necessary intermediate stage on the road toward a genuine socialism or communism, imposed by the economic conditions of Russia and by the fact that socialism could not exist in only one country surrounded by hostile capitalist powers. Later socialist and communist leaders, from Joseph Stalin onwards, declared that the state capitalism they had achieved and were administering was already much more than that: it was a form of socialism or even communism. The difficulties and obstacles to moving beyond state capitalism were thus made even more challenging by insistent decla-

---

* A complete elaboration of this argument, as well as its systematic application to the rise and fall of the Soviet Union, is available in Resnick and Wolff, *Class Theory and History*. See also Satyananda J. Gabriel, *Chinese Capitalism and the Modernist Vision* (New York: Routledge, 2005).

rations that the move had been accomplished. The skeptics who doubted that accomplishment or openly spoke of the differences between state capitalism and socialism were quickly banished to the margins of allowable social opinion—or worse.

However, from our perspective, none of the actually existing socialist countries has so far been able to develop much beyond state capitalism, no matter how insistently and persistently they called their societies socialist or communist. Thus, struggles that were fought as pitting capitalism against socialism were actually conflicts among relatively more and less regulated private and state capitalisms.

What happened in most "actually existing" socialist or communist economies followed logically from the beliefs of the people who won power there. The more moderate leaders, usually called "socialist," achieved transitions from unregulated or lightly regulated private capitalisms to heavily regulated private capitalisms. Many modern "social democracies" fit that depiction. The less moderate leaders, usually called "communist," achieved transitions from unregulated or lightly regulated private capitalisms to full state capitalism, in which the state took over large portions—or at least the "commanding heights"—of the country's industrial enterprises. In both cases, the internal organization of the vast majority of industrial enterprises remained capitalist. The productive workers continued in all cases to produce surpluses: they added more in value by their labor than what they received in return for that labor. Their surpluses were in all cases appropriated and distributed by others.

In short, capitalism, socialism, and communism as they were understood and actually existed over the last century shared a common organization of the surplus in their industries. That organization was capitalist. It was not—or at least not yet—an organization in which the producers and appropriators/distributors of the surplus were the same people. The great debate between capitalism and socialism, the debate that so many (Francis Fukuyama, Robert L. Heilbroner, and others) had declared finally resolved in capitalism's favor by the 1990s, turns out to have been a debate between private and state capitalism.

Within actually existing socialist states there have been greater and lesser movements back toward private capitalism over the last half-century. Many social reforms achieved as part of the movements toward socialism after 1917 proved temporary and subject to erosion or reversal. Especially after the 1980s, socialized property in the means of production reverted to private property. Planning apparatuses gave way to market mechanisms of distribution. Relatively more economic and social equality returned to greater inequality. To the millions who struggled for socialism and communism over the last 150 years, who believed them to be embodiments of a more egalitarian and democratic social order, the last several decades of movement back toward private capitalism have been deeply distressing and demoralizing.

5.4 Socialism and Democracy

The lesson I draw, however, is rather different. The problem that prevented actually existing socialisms and communisms from becoming more egalitarian, democratic societies was precisely their state capitalist organization of production. The socialists who led those societies had not prioritized or even understood the reorganization of production necessary to make a transition from capitalism to a different economic system. A few, like Lenin, did, but their utterly new experiences of power, the dangerous internal and external oppositions they faced, and their urgent needs to revive production for the very survival of the new socialist administrations were among pressing conditions that made the reorganization of production seem important but less pressing than other priorities. This meant that existing socialist societies were, like private capitalist societies, undemocratic and marked by social inequalities. In socialist societies, too, the exclusion of the mass of workers from directing their workplaces produced alienation and nurtured resentment. There was a general disinclination to take responsibility for social developments in the broader communities, for economic development generally, or even for the immediate circumstances of one's workplace and residence. Exclusion from economic decision-making on the job seemed to lead many workers to refuse or exclude themselves from community decision-making elsewhere.

In private capitalism, the capitalist organization of production renders political democracy a mere formality without substance. That same organization of production limited socialist societies, whatever their initial egalitarian and democratic achievements for the mass of citizens. In the end, when major crises hit these societies in the 1980s and their state apparatuses could not contain or manage them, the mass of people could imagine no other option than a transition back toward private capitalism. The prevalent way of defining and differentiating actually existing socialism—in terms of private versus socialized property and markets versus planning—was shared by its friends and foes. When severe crisis hit state capitalism, the only conceivable alternative for nearly everyone was another oscillation to private capitalism and a rejection of "socialism."

A few left-wing socialists and communists tried to challenge the framework of oscillations among private and state capitalisms understood as socialisms. They often advocated instead transitions from actually existing socialism to genuinely democratic socialism in which social ownership and planning coexisted with democratic political structures and practices such as liberalizing civil liberties, allowing multiple political parties, and so on. Once again, however, the focus was on adding political democracy to a system already socialist by virtue of social ownership and planning. These socialists paid far less attention to (and thus offered few specifics on) how to ground a socialist political democracy on an economic democracy quite different from what prevailed in actually existing socialist economies.

I take a different view: there is an essential connection between the radical reorganization of production and real democracy. Achieving the latter requires a transition from a capitalist to the workers' self-directed system I describe in the remaining chapters of this book. Only when real democracy is established on the job, only when we institute economic democracy, can we expect or build a democratic politics. Part III of this book explores precisely the needed reorganization of production—democracy at work.

My proposal of democracy at work is also a cure for the failures of actually existing socialisms. All of the varieties of state socialism in the twentieth century discovered that their progressive reforms—universal health care; public education; subsidized food, housing, daycare, and transportation; guaranteed employment; and so on—were not permanent, not part of the historically necessary transition from capitalism to communism. The economic and political base of massive popular support for those reforms was not sufficiently strong to make them irreversible. One reason for that insufficient strength was the social divisions provoked and sustained by undemocratic capitalist workplaces, by the tensions and conflicts between the producers and appropriators of the surplus in production, who belonged to different social groups. When crises hit state socialist regimes, those tensions and conflicts produced imbalanced, ineffective government interventions that heightened social divisions and encouraged the idea that private capitalism offered the best solution to the problems of socialism (state capitalism).

The twentieth century has rendered a profound verdict on the old debate between reform and revolution. Many in this debate had long seen these as alternative strategies for social progress (though many, such as Rosa Luxemburg, and before her Marx and Engels, saw them as intertwined). In the 1930s, for example, reformers believed that the best achievable response to the Great Depression was the set of New Deal reforms implemented by President Roosevelt. In contrast, revolutionaries advocated a variety of structural economic transformations that would go further than Roosevelt's more regulated private capitalism. Likewise, in Russia, the 1917 revolution established many reforms, but the revolutionaries who wanted to transform society more profoundly were ultimately defeated. In short, reformers prevailed over revolutionaries almost everywhere.

Yet half a century later, the reforms achieved—after much social struggle—have proved insecure, vulnerable, and reversible. Securing the sorts of reforms achieved in the twentieth century by advocates of regulated capitalism, socialism, and communism requires doing more, going further than reformers anywhere have understood. To secure these reforms requires revolutionary changes.

Reformers and revolutionaries need not and should not be adversaries. Indeed, one goal of this book's arguments for democracy at work—a reorganization of production that goes well beyond "reform"—is to lay out a program for revolutionary change that can achieve reforms that won't easily be reversed.

5.5 A Concluding Parable

In conclusion, I want to offer a parable that sums up my argument in this chapter. Modern-day socialists are somewhat like the antislavery activists of the mid-nineteenth century. Antislavery agitators split into two subgroups. The first, horrified by slavery, chose to agitate for improvements in slaves' diets, clothing, housing, the treatment of their families, and so on. A second group of antislavery activists agreed with the first group's demands and goals, but was also bitterly angry with them about the limitations of their politics. They insisted that the basic problem of slavery was slavery itself, not merely the living conditions of the slaves. Even if reforms in the conditions of slaves might be won, so long as they remained slaves, those reforms would be insecure and reversible. This more radical group—the abolitionists—insisted that slavery would have to be dissolved in favor of universal personal freedom and emancipation.

Modern anticapitalist socialists and communists have split similarly into two subgroups. The reformers have agitated for better wages and working conditions, protective laws, economic regulations, and so on. They demand better treatment for wage and salary earners. Revolutionaries agree with those demands, yet also denounce their limits. For example, as I have shown above, even if such reforms are achieved (as they were by the mass struggles of the CIO, socialists, and communists in the 1930s), they will remain insecure and reversible so long as nothing is done about the workers' subordination to capitalists. The capitalist organization of production must now be dissolved. Workers must become their own directors, receiving and distributing the surpluses they produce. They must become the collective decision-makers in productive enterprises, no longer the directed wage and salary receivers.

Slaves had finally to become their own masters to move society beyond the inhumanity, inequality, and indignity of slavery. Wage and salary earners have likewise to become their own directors, to move society beyond the inhumanity, inequality, and indignity of capitalism in all its myriad forms.

Part III:
Workers' Self-Directed Enterprises as a Cure

The world is at a crossroads. It is struggling with the second major collapse of private capitalism in seventy-five years—this one far more global than the last. Criticism of private capitalism and opposition to it are growing everywhere. Opposition to its traditional rival—the state capitalism that so many considered to be socialism—ended Soviet and Eastern European socialisms and now challenges the remaining state capitalisms that call themselves socialist. Dissatisfaction with the two major economic systems in the world—private and state capitalisms—is provoking a search for a real alternative to both of them.

Stale arguments and ineffective programs meant to salvage more or less regulated private capitalism leave critics unmoved. Why focus on regulations and other government economic interventions when all of post-1930s history shows how hollow and reversible they are? Likewise, why support a transition to state capitalism (whether or not it is called "socialism") when such past efforts solved only a few of private capitalism's basic problems, suppressed political democracy as much as or more than private capitalism, and proved as vulnerable to severe crises?

At the same time, the collapse of Soviet and Eastern European actually existing socialisms and partial turns toward private capitalism elsewhere (especially in China) have left a profound legacy. The attractiveness, durability, and viability of traditional socialism have been challenged. Large numbers of people in formerly socialist societies that reverted back to private capitalism seem determined not to oscillate back again, even when they experience private capitalism's stark crises, failures, and injustices.

So long as the critics of private capitalism cannot specify an alternative other than a more regulated private capitalism or state capitalism (traditional socialism), they will not inspire or mobilize a social movement able to break out of repeated oscillations between them. So long as the critics of actually existing socialism offer no better alternatives than reversion to private capitalism or state capitalism "with more democracy," they will not organize such a movement, either. Working classes will respond to both critics, as they already have implicitly: "No, thank you, we have been there and done that already. It is a dead end."

Serious critics of capitalism need to present and champion the goal of a new economic system different from and beyond both private and state capitalism if we are to inspire and build the social movement now needed. Going beyond the now-exhausted oscillations between private and state capitalisms requires a clear understanding of their limits, rooted in their shared organization of production. It requires a genuinely different organization of productive enterprises: workers' self-directed enterprises. The following chapters explain their workings and explore their virtues.

6 What "Self-Directed" Means

To define a workers' self-directed enterprise (WSDE), I will begin by contrasting it with a modern private capitalist corporation. In that corporation, shareholders vote, one vote per share, to determine who will compose the board of directors (usually between nine and twenty people). Those persons are almost never workers inside the corporation. A few board members are sometimes also a corporation's very top managers. This board then collectively appropriates and distributes the surplus (roughly the revenue net of direct production costs) generated inside the corporation. This board also decides what commodities to produce, how to produce them, what technology to utilize, and where to locate their production and distribution facilities. Finally, the board chooses and hires both the management and the workers in the enterprise.

Often—nearly always, in larger corporations—a very few major shareholders own a controlling bloc of shares. That is, they collectively have the dominant shareholder voice or power. They select the members of the corporation's board of directors. If the major shareholders are displeased with the board's decisions, they can change the board's composition.

By contrast, in a WSDE, no separate group of persons—no individual who does not participate in the productive work of the enterprise—can be a member of the board of directors. Even if there were to be shareholders of a WDSE, they would not have the power to elect the directors. Instead, all of the workers who produce the surplus generated inside the enterprise function collectively to appropriate and distribute it. They alone compose the board of directors.

This is what I mean by self-directed. As I will explain in more detail below, the workers collectively determine what the enterprise produces, the appropriate technology, the location of production, and related matters. They do this in conjunction—in a shared democratic decision-making process—with the surrounding communities at the local, regional, and national levels.

In a state capitalist enterprise, the board of directors is typically a specific set of state officials. They collectively appropriate the surpluses produced in the industrial enterprises they direct. The Soviet Council of Ministers, for example, functioned as a kind of centralized capitalist board of directors, the parallel structure to the board of directors of a private capitalist corporate conglomerate. There the state functioned, in effect, as the sole shareholder representing the ownership of socialized productive industrial assets.

Of course, instead of such centralized state capitalism, there could be decentralized state capitalism. In that case, the appropriation and distribution of surpluses is delegated to lower levels of state officials who direct less-aggregated units of industrial production.

Both state and private capitalisms have periodically experimented with more- and less-centralized appropriation and distribution of surpluses.

The basic difference between both private and state capitalist economic systems and the alternative system built upon WSDEs is that only in the latter do the workers who produce the surpluses collectively appropriate and distribute those surpluses. However, before detailing how WSDEs would work internally or how they would interact with one another, consumers, and surrounding communities, we need to differentiate WSDEs from worker-owned enterprises, worker-managed enterprises, and cooperatives generally.

6.1 Worker-Owned Enterprises

When workers partly or completely own the corporate enterprises in which they work, they occupy a position like that of other shareholders within private capitalism. In most cases, shareholders have two key functions: they elect the directors of the enterprise and they receive portions of the appropriated surplus from the directors as dividends. Owners of shares in capitalist corporations are usually passive relative to the directors. Under US law, for example, it is the prerogative of the board of directors to determine what portion of appropriated surplus is distributed as dividends to owners. They are free to distribute none, as is often the case. In effect, owners of shares have only the power to change directors at annual elections. The key capitalist roles—directing production and appropriating and distributing the surplus—are played by the directors of capitalist enterprises, not by their owners.

Employee stock ownership plans (ESOPs) have been established in various enterprises across the landscape of US capitalism.

Comparable worker-ownership programs exist in many other countries as well. Sometimes they have been instituted from below. For example, workers have sometimes prevented an enterprise from closing by buying it themselves and maintaining production. Sometimes they have been instituted by private capitalists seeking workers to buy an enterprise no other capitalist wants or to pay a price no other capitalist will. Sometimes state authorities intervene to establish worker-owned enterprises. In any of these cases, when ownership changes from private individuals outside the enterprise to the workers inside, partly or totally, it is very different from a change in the direction of the enterprise.

If workers become owners of a capitalist corporate enterprise, they have the right to elect as members of the board of directors persons other than themselves. They usually do that and leave the directing of the enterprise to those directors, much as nonworker shareholders typically do. It might be legally possible for worker-owners to transform the enterprise so that they become not only owners but also, collectively, directors. However, that has very rarely happened. Worker-owned enterprises are thus conceptually and also empirically different from WSDEs.

6.2 Worker-Managed Enterprises

The difference is even more marked between worker-managed enterprises and WSDEs. Management is a different function from directing in private and state capitalist corporations. Typically, corporate boards of directors search for, select, hire, and remunerate managers. A managerial chain of command is established and its top levels (such as the CEO) report regularly to the board of directors on the managers' execution of the board's basic directions. The function of managers is to monitor, supervise, and control both the production of commodities inside capitalist enterprises and all of the ancillary nonproduction tasks needed to achieve profits and growth (purchasing of inputs, sales of outputs, legal counsel, advertising, lobbying, and so on). Under worker-managed enterprises, workers who perform managerial functions do not thereby displace capitalists or move the economy beyond capitalism. Workers who self-manage (for example, to secure more control over the forms and pace of their labor process) still function to execute the basic enterprise decisions made elsewhere by the directors. Capitalists have sometimes given or urged management functions onto workers. That can make management cheaper by saving the cost of professional managers; it can also make management more effective, because workers prefer self-management to management by others. In sum, under worker-managed enterprises, capitalists give the workers more control over the work in the hope of receiving in turn more profits or growth. It is possible that workers who gain experience in management might want to use that to agitate for positions on an enterprise's board of directors—or even take it over. Then a WSDE could emerge. However, that has very rarely happened. Conceptually and empirically, workers' self-management, like workers' ownership, is different from WSDEs.

Because socialism and workers' self-management have been historically associated with each other and have often been treated as if they were identical, it is especially important to clarify their differences. Workers' self-management and workers' self-direction are very different ways to reorganize productive enterprises. Whatever its virtues may be, workers' self-management has mostly served private or state capitalism. Historically, experiments in workers' self-management (for example, at Volvo in Sweden) have ended when they no longer served the interests of their capitalist directors. In contrast, WSDEs represent a social transition beyond capitalism.

6.3 Cooperatives

The term "cooperative" (or "co-op") has a very long history in many countries and has been used to describe a broad range of institutions and enterprises. Cooperative ownership, cooperative purchasing, cooperative selling, and cooperative labor have all been called co-ops. None of these, whatever their virtues, has any necessary connection with WSDEs. For example, groups of farmers have sometimes purchased and cooperatively owned land together, while each has hired workers and farmed a portion of the cooperatively owned land as a capitalist enterprise. In this case, co-op refers to how the land is owned, but not to the organization of production or class structure of the farming enterprise. Similarly, groups of small capitalist enterprises producing software products may cooperatively purchase certain inputs they all need, perhaps sharing their use. That would mean capitalist enterprises forming a purchasing co-op among themselves. For centuries, groups of small and medium-sized capitalist enterprises within the same industry have banded together into sales or marketing co-ops to secure higher prices than they would command individually. But none of these are WSDEs.

Even cooperative labor is something different from a WSDE. In nearly all capitalist enterprises, hired workers perform labor cooperatively. What distinguishes the WSDE is therefore not cooperative labor. Rather, two facts define WSDEs: that the appropriation and distribution of the surplus are done cooperatively and that the workers who cooperatively produce the surplus and those who cooperatively appropriate and distribute it are identical.

7 How WSDEs Work Internally

Periodically, in any WSDE, the collective of workers that produces a surplus gathers to collectively receive that surplus and distribute it. The surplus is never appropriated and distributed by others. WSDEs are, to make use of Marx's precise term, nonexploitative organizations (class structures) of production because they do not involve one group of people appropriating the surplus produced by another. That is how WSDEs differ from the exploitative class structures of capitalist, feudal, and slave production systems.

Capitalism's champions take pride in differentiating it from slavery and feudalism. Capitalism, they say, is based on free contracts between free individuals. It rejects the unfreedom of slaves—individuals who belong, as property, to others—and of serfs—individuals tied by custom or tradition to produce surplus for a particular feudal lord. But capitalism shares with slavery and feudalism a common basic feature.

123

Capitalism, like slavery and feudalism, is also exploitative. In contrast, WSDEs represent, finally, freedom from exploitation: slave, feudal, and capitalist.

In WSDEs, each productive worker's job description not only includes the specific tasks that he or she performs within an enterprise's division of surplus-producing labor but also requires each worker to participate equally in democratic decision-making by the enterprise's board of directors. Each productive worker is an equal member of that board. The collective of such workers constitutes the board.

As such a board, productive workers collectively carry out the social distribution of the surpluses they have produced and appropriated. They use this surplus partly to pay taxes to the various levels of government that provide them with certain conditions of their existence. They use another portion of the surplus to hire and provide operating budgets as needed to managers, clerks, security guards, lawyers, and other workers not directly engaged in producing surpluses but crucial in other ways to reproducing the enterprise.* The board distributes the portions of the surplus used to expand production (invest and grow), paid in dividends to owners of the enterprise, used to lobby state officials, and so on.

---

* Marx called these other workers "unproductive laborers," chiefly to distinguish them from those ("productive laborers") whose labor directly produces the surplus. As argued elsewhere (see Resnick and Wolff, *Knowledge and Class*, chapter 3), Marx explicitly stressed that unproductive laborers are as crucial to reproducing capitalist class structures as productive laborers. However, critics of Marx's arguments and even some of his followers have read "unproductive" as if Marx meant to denigrate or render secondary such labor and such laborers. So I will avoid using that term within the substantive analysis of the two kinds of workers within WSDEs in favor of a new terminology, as presented below in Section 7.1 of this chapter.

In reaching its decisions regarding the distribution of the surplus, the board must contend with, accommodate, and reach compromises with others. Thus, for example, the portion of the surplus that the board must distribute to the state as taxes is influenced by state officials, by cultural attitudes toward government, and so on. Many different social groups wield influence or power over the distribution of all the portions of the surplus alongside that wielded by the board. However, the board alone performs the distribution.

One key goal of the distribution of the surplus is typically to secure the reproduction of the WSDE. WSDEs, individually and as a group, recognize the need for all sorts of social supports if they are to survive and succeed. They must distribute portions of their surpluses to secure such supports. For example, for collectives of surplus-producing workers to effectively direct their enterprises, the workers will need the appropriate education and training for themselves and for children coming after them. They may decide to entrust such education and training to public schools sustained partly or entirely by taxes on their surpluses. They will be concerned that such schools have curricula that stress the techniques and attitudes needed for collective, democratic decision-making as central to economic activity and social welfare. Public education thus would likely be very different in an economic system based on WSDEs rather than capitalism.

To take another example, the board of a WSDE would likely see the need to secure certain management functions. It might, like its capitalist counterparts, hire professional managers. On the other hand, it might prefer instead, for many reasons, to substitute a rotational system whereby all surplus-producing workers are periodically rotated through management positions. The board might see this as an appropriate way to avoid reifying people into fixed positions of manager and managed—positions that might possibly pave the way for a return to capitalism. Workers who were thus temporarily removed from producing surpluses would nonetheless need to be funded for their management activities and time by the board's distributions from the surplus it appropriates from the nonmanagerial workers. The extent to which worker-directors are also rotated through management functions would further differentiate a WSDE-based economy from capitalism.

To take a final example, consider that an economic system built upon WSDEs might well be generally concerned about slipping back toward a capitalist system. To that end, it would seek to avoid crises or cycles of the sorts caused in capitalism by overproduction, underconsumption, technological unemployment, and so on. It would work to overcome the social problems created under capitalism when an enterprise discovers a new way to produce output with less labor input, encounters a loss of public desire for its products, or finds that it has overestimated the demand for its output. One way to accomplish this would be to create a fund (by surplus distributions from WSDE boards) and a government agency to administer it. Any WSDE that faced a need to lay off workers would qualify for assistance. The agency would survey and interview workers to determine those most interested in new and different jobs. It could provide needed training, relocation, and other services to effect employment changes from enterprises and industries needing fewer workers to those seeking expansion. In this way, unemployment would be eliminated without compromising various incentives for labor-saving technological progress and without ignoring changing patterns of citizens' demands for certain goods and services. A system based on WSDEs would secure its social position and support by such solutions to the problems of technical change and shifting demand patterns that have so often provoked or worsened economic cycles and crises in capitalism.

Inventors and innovators in a WSDE-based economic system would, like their counterparts in capitalist systems, face problems to solve and incentives to realize the production of new goods or services. Funds would have to be secured (from public agencies provided with surplus allocations from existing WSDEs and/or from private sources that could include individuals and other WSDEs) when the inventors and innovators did not have sufficient funds of their own. Workers would have to be gathered who would leave existing employments to help start and staff the new WSDE. Similarly, incentives would have to be established, such as tax considerations, temporarily higher personal incomes for the worker/directors in successful new WSDEs, social recognition and rewards, and so on. Interestingly, the WSDE-based system would not need a patent system (nor suffer its constraint on other people's use of new inventions), since it could provide alternative incentives for innovation just as it established alternative sources of needed funding.

To end most exploitative organizations of production and establish instead a system based on WSDEs is a basic and foundational social change. Such a change cannot happen alone or in isolation from a host of other social changes. Those other social changes are either prerequisites for WSDEs to be established or they are changes that WSDEs will encourage and support to reproduce, secure, and expand themselves. It is thus an error to think about the emergence of WSDEs as if everything else in the societies where capitalism prevails would remain the same.

Both the long-term features of capitalist economic systems and the crisis conditions they produced in 2007 have opened up new possibilities for a movement toward WSDEs as the basis of an alternative economic system. If WSDEs emerge and come to a prominent position within modern capitalist economies, they will need to change many social conditions to be able to survive, expand, and secure mass support. Redesigning the curricula in schools, rotating workers through management positions, reorganizing sources and incentives for productive innovation, and creating an effective program to avoid unemployment are all examples of changes produced by WSDEs. Indeed, concrete steps toward these goals have been achieved over the last fifty years by the Mondragón Corporation in Spain, which now includes eighty-five thousand members in its constituent worker cooperative enterprises.

7.1 The Two Kinds of Workers in Every WSDE

We are now ready to tackle a particularly thorny issue in the analysis of an economic system based on WSDEs. This concerns the division of the employees of every WSDE into two groups with different relationships to the production and distribution of the surplus. The first group comprises the workers who produce surpluses and who also compose the board of directors in WSDEs. They are the workers who directly produce the outputs of the WSDEs—the software programs, shirts, buses, machines, and so on. Every WSDE also employs another, different kind of worker who provides the conditions and ancillary services that enable the surplus-producers to function. I will call these workers enablers.

Enablers include the secretaries, clerks, receptionists, security guards, cleaning staff, and so on who maintain the paperwork and physical spaces that provide the necessary conditions for the first group of workers to produce a surplus. Other types of enablers include managers, lawyers, architects, and counselors who provide still other conditions.

Enablers are just as crucial for the reproduction of the WSDE as are the surplus-producers. However, unlike the surplus-producing workers, enablers do not directly produce the surplus; rather, they provide various conditions for the surplus-producers to function effectively. The enabling group of workers obtains its sustenance and the means to perform its functions by receiving distributed shares of the surplus from the worker-directors. In other words, the surplus-producers need the enablers to be able to produce surpluses, while the enablers need surplus distributions from the surplus-producers/appropriators to be able to perform their enabling functions.

To survive, then, WSDEs must work out mutually acceptable relationships between the two kinds of workers. The enablers and the surplus-producers must together and democratically answer the following questions: (1) how much surplus will be produced, appropriated, and thus be available for distribution and (2) what portions of that surplus will be distributed to secure which conditions of surplus production provided by which distinct subgroup of enablers. There will be contradictions to resolve, areas of agreement and also of disagreement among and between surplus-producers and enablers.

The end of exploitation—a defining point and purpose of WSDEs—requires that the producers of the surplus be identical to the appropriators and distributors. However—this is a key consideration—that does not require excluding the enablers from full democratic participation with the surplus-producers in deciding the size and specific distribution of the surplus. The power to decide the size and distribution of the surplus is democratically shared by all of the workers in a WSDE. The physical processes of appropriating and distributing the surplus are reserved for the subset of surplus-producing workers.

In summary, the two different kinds of workers are interdependent.

They are both required for the WSDE to survive. They each determine key components of the work activity and the incomes of the other. Their need to work out and constantly adjust their relationship democratically will profoundly shape WSDEs' internal life as well as distinguish it from the internal life of the capitalist enterprise.

7.2 Handling Technical Change

WSDEs would handle typical economic challenges in a manner quite different from capitalist enterprises. Suppose an affordable new technology emerges that allows an enterprise to produce more output with considerably less labor and little change in other inputs. In private capitalist enterprises, such technological advances are usually implemented by innovating boards of directors, unless they are blocked or altered by labor unions. Surpluses accruing to the innovating private capitalist enterprise rise and some laborers get laid off.

In this example, the beneficiaries of the technical change—the board of directors of the private capitalist enterprise—are also the decision-makers. Those bearing the costs of the technical change— the laid-off workers, their families, and communities (including other private capitalists)—are excluded from the decisions about technological change. The net social costs or benefits of the technical change are indeterminate.* However, the injustices of the decision-making process and of its likely outcomes are quite clear.

From the history of state capitalist economies—at least of those whose supporters believed them to be "socialist"—we know that

---

* One might be tempted to ask whether the social benefits of installing the new technology are greater or less than the costs flowing from the unemployment of technical changes posed a different problem. State capitalist enterprises were less driven by market competition to install new technologies or else disappear (as compared to private capitalist enterprises). At the same time, their socialist dimensions and political context committed them to maintaining employment as a kind of basic human right. Thus, state capitalist enterprises typically developed their technologies more slowly than their private capitalist counterparts. Their slower technical advances helped to undermine state capitalism because, on an international scale, they were competing with economies based on private capitalism.

WSDEs would manage such technical changes differently. In contrast to private capitalist enterprises, the decision to install the new technology would involve a much larger and more diverse collection of decision-makers. To allocate a portion of the enterprise's surplus to purchase and install the new technology would be a decision that surplus-producers and enablers would have to reach together democratically. Instead of a dozen or so board members making that decision, hundreds or thousands of workers would participate. Unlike capitalist firms, the decisions of WSDEs would take into account a much larger set of concerns about the impacts of a proposed technical change not only on the surplus but on its distribution and on workers, their families, and the surrounding communities in which the workers live and with which the WSDEs interact.

The net costs or benefits of the technological decision reached

---

the laborers and its social impacts. Insurmountable difficulties confront anyone seeking to identify and measure all the benefits and costs of technical change (no one has ever yet managed to do that). In any case, in private capitalism, typically, authoritative agencies rarely even try to make such measurements. Instead it is an endlessly repeated article of capitalist faith that the system's technical "progress" yields more benefits than costs.

by a WSDE—like those of capitalist enterprises—remain unknown (and unknowable), but the democratic and social justice dimensions of these deliberations are vastly improved. In contrast to the often conservative technological decisions of state-capitalist enterprises, WSDEs would manage the interaction between technical change and job security differently. A specialized agency would need to be established that would immediately swing into action upon learning of an enterprise considering a labor-saving technical change. It would always know, from constant monitoring, which existing enterprises need more laborers, which have registered that wish to commence new production, all the relevant skill and experience requirements, and where affected laborers and enterprises are located. Rather like a matchmaking service, this agency's task would be to match employees willing to change jobs with job availability and to arrange for appropriate training and inducements to facilitate the reallocation of personnel. No loss of income would attend the transition period for workers who left one job for another. To run this agency would cost a small portion of all the surpluses distributed by WSDEs to sustain its staff and activities. This agency's reports and services would form one basis for the decision by all workers about whether to make the technical change in question.

Finally, consider the incentive to innovate technically. Invention and innovation in private and state capitalist enterprises is slowed or blocked by workers who fear that they will participate minimally in the gains from and maximally in the costs of installing the technical change. In an economy based on WSDEs, the gains and costs would be shared across the totality of employees in ways they would democratically establish. For example, periodically, debates would be arranged and votes taken as to how to share the gains in productivity (what combination of greater leisure for workers or greater quantities of output). Since workers in WSDEs decide the size and distribution of surpluses, that includes deciding whether and when to use a portion of their appropriated surpluses to purchase and install technical changes. In capitalism, where workers are excluded from choices about technology, they choose between labor and leisure based on the wage given by their competition in the labor market. In contrast, workers in WSDEs make their labor/leisure choice together with and as part of their decisions about technological change.

The quantity, pace, and quality of technical advance would differ from that in capitalist economic systems. The historic promise of capitalists—that their technical innovations would eventuate in less labor time and more leisure for the mass of people—has never been kept. In the contemporary United States, for example, more family members are working more hours of paid labor than ever before in US history and, likewise, more than workers in virtually all other countries. The sizable gains in productivity of which capitalism's celebrants boast have accrued instead as rising surpluses and profits to those who decide about technology: the capitalists, not the workers.

7.3 Handling Environmental Issues

The modern histories of private and state capitalist economic systems offer many examples of their capitalist enterprises' failures to take into account the environmental impacts and costs of their decisions. Both forms of capitalist enterprises routinely use technologies with negative and costly impacts on their workers' physical and mental health as well as harmful effects on surrounding communities. They also choose to produce outputs and utilize inputs with the same drawbacks. The ways in which enterprises define and maintain the quality of air, water, temperature, humidity, noise, and so on in the workplace are typically undertaken without adequate—or any—regard for their surrounding impact on the short- and long-term well-being of people in the enterprise or their communities.

A root of this problem is the small number of people directing private and state capitalist enterprises, who are often located far from the site of enterprise production, and the goals and incentives driving them. Competitive survival, profitability, growth, and market share drive private capitalist enterprises; those goals comprise their bottom-line concerns. Fulfilling government production plans, increasing surpluses, holding reserves to offset planning shortages and errors, and so on drive state capitalist enterprises. From the standpoint of both systems, environmental concern is typically a luxury that private and state capitalists believe they cannot afford.

WSDEs would approach environmental issues quite differently. First and foremost, workers live, play, and raise families in and around their sites of work. For them the costs of environmental degradation are a much more important and immediate consideration than for a small group of outside capitalist directors who have enough wealth to avoid living or working in places vulnerable to environmental degradation and its effects. The bottom-line objectives of private and state capitalists would be subordinated to environmental considerations in WSDEs' decisions. We cannot know the net costs or benefits of, for example, less investment in new capital and labor power for growth coupled with more investment in improving the natural environment of enterprise work. But we can know that environmental concerns are far more likely to be raised and counted in reaching decisions in a WSDE.

7.4 Handling the Distribution of Incomes and of Jobs

One of the conditions for the long-term survival of WSDEs is greater democracy in the noneconomic parts of society. Likewise, real (as opposed to merely formal) democracy in communities and the larger society is tenuous, if not impossible, without economic democracy inside enterprises. Genuinely shared and democratic decision-making by workers in WSDEs requires limits on the different resources each individual worker brings to such decisions. To pay some workers many times more than others or to compensate some workers so poorly that they need three jobs and have neither time nor energy to participate in politics or workplace deliberations would undermine and eventually dissolve WSDEs.

Thus, a system based on WSDEs and reproducing them over time would likely mandate minimum and maximum income levels for all workers, based on democratically chosen criteria. Within those boundaries, WSDEs could determine and adjust their schedules of wages and salaries. WSDEs would not likely support or allow the individual income disparities found in private or state capitalism. The Spanish workers' cooperatives gathered in the Mondragón Corporation have also achieved important steps in this direction. This would be the case partly because the survival of the WSDE as such would require far lower income disparities. It would also be the case because democracy in politics outside the WSDEs requires far narrower income disparities than characterize capitalism (especially private capitalism, but also often state capitalism).

Reducing income disparities in an economic system based on WSDEs can return an old issue—rotation of work—to the forefront of social agendas for change. Income differences can be reduced by narrowing the differences in wages and salaries assigned to specific jobs in an enterprise's division of labor. Alternatively, the same result can be achieved by rotating workers regularly through a variety of jobs to which different wages or salaries have been assigned. In a WSDE-type system, workers in each WSDE could rotate through nondirectorial jobs while always also serving as equal members of the collective board of directors.

For the reproduction of an economic system based upon WSDEs, such a job rotation system would have many benefits. First, repeating one particular job within a division of labor for a lifetime or even for years does not develop a broad range of different experiences and competencies. Yet that broad range is precisely what would best prepare each worker to evaluate options and make the decisions involved in directing an enterprise. Second, performing different jobs sequentially enables a particular "learning by doing" to develop. Workers do not necessarily know what kinds of work they do best or by which they are most personally satisfied. It certainly might not be their first job. Moreover, which jobs most engage people's skills and enthusiasm can change across a lifetime. Finally, specific jobs also change with technical and social conditions.

Rotating workers through jobs can address these issues far more effectively than has been accomplished by private and state capitalism. Rotating workers more broadly to learn their preferences and areas of greater productivity among jobs, and then perhaps rotating them more narrowly among just those jobs, would achieve not only a more egalitarian income distribution but also a more effective distribution of jobs. Moreover, room can be left for each enterprise to decide the periods of time assigned to each job based on criteria such as the job's arduousness, how long it takes to develop or improve the appropriate job skills, and so on. Within the larger economy, to induce workers to shift into certain industries (for example, because of the technical or environmental considerations), the WSDEs within such industries might pay higher than usual wages and salaries for an initial period. Such temporary pay increases could come from a fund for that purpose derived from a portion of all WSDEs' surpluses.

A WSDE-based economic system could thus address the ancient problems of the division of labor and specialization of function. Adam Smith's pin factory has often been interpreted as a rationalization for ever-more-narrow specialization of jobs, training, and mentalities as necessary for maximizing surpluses and profits. For most of those interpretations, specialization of a function has been treated as identical to specialization of the functionary. Yet that is not the case. Whatever the merits of specialization of function within a division of labor, the merits of equivalently specializing the laborer are dubious. Beyond a certain degree and a certain period of time, keeping one person in one job may reduce productivity and profitability. If a fully rounded personality and a diversely engaged body and mind are connected to personal happiness, genuine democracy, and work productivity, then a WSDE-based economic system with rotation of jobs will be far more fulfilling—and quite possibly more productive—than work has been under private or state capitalism.

8 Property Ownership, Markets, Planning, and the Efficiency Myth

Because of the historical association between socialism and various notions of collectivized workplaces, I will focus first in this chapter on the connection between socialism and WSDEs. Building on the discussion in chapter 5, recall that traditionally, socialism has mostly been differentiated from capitalism in terms of socialized (or nationalized) property in means of production rather than private property and in terms of central government planning rather than markets as means of distributing productive resources and products. In chapter 5, I argued that such differentiations marginalized or ignored the transformation of the internal organization of enterprises—and particularly of the production, appropriation, and distribution of the surplus.

8.1 Macro-Level and Micro-Level Transformations

Among socialists themselves—and even among Marxists presumably familiar with Marx's focus on the production, appropriation, and distribution of the surplus in all three volumes of his *Capital*—the focus on state ownership and planning has always been remarkable. There were always some who did see the need for microeconomic transformation inside enterprises, envisioning various forms of more direct control by workers, not mediated or distorted by government or party. Yet they rarely concretized those forms in specific terms of the surplus, speaking more often in general terms of direct democracy. Moreover, the practical exigencies of the USSR after 1917 and of "actually existing socialist" economies thereafter led them to emphasize expanding output (and especially means of production) via state ownership and planning. This too helped to push issues of radical transformation inside enterprises to a very secondary status, especially among those who equated socialism with what those economies were struggling to establish. They often banished notions of workers becoming also the direct, first appropriators and hence distributors of enterprise surpluses to the murky future realms of socialist utopias.

In my view, the macro-level changes brought about by traditional socialism (nationalized ownership of means of production, planning, reduced income inequality, etc.) did not survive in part because they were not accompanied and reinforced by micro-level changes in the internal reorganization of enterprises. A viable and durable socialism requires both micro- and macro-level transformations of capitalism. That is a major lesson of the first century of efforts to establish and build socialism.

My micro-level focus does not simplistically respond to traditional socialism's overemphasis on the macro level by an overemphasis of the micro level. The point is rather to integrate the two levels in theory and in practice to yield a new conception and practice of socialism that can better critique and challenge capitalism in the twenty-first century.

8.2 Ownership of WSDEs

To deepen this analysis, let's consider the ownership of the means of production. Various ownership arrangements can coexist with WSDEs. The state might own the means and make them available to WSDEs. If so, the arrangement might involve only centralized state ownership or perhaps some mixture of state, regional, and local governments owning various kinds and quantities of productive property. Alternatively, instead of the state, the workers within the WSDE could themselves own the productive property they use in the production process. They could do so collectively or individually. Finally, ownership of productive property could be conventionally private and chiefly individual; for example, ownership could take the form of shares traded on a market, and so on.

The salient point is that the internal organization of surplus production, appropriation, and distribution in WSDEs is different from and can coexist with various forms of ownership of means of production. Whichever property ownership system WSDEs coexist and interact with will affect their evolution (their viability, durability, and so on). In the case of a traditional socialism that begins to integrate WSDEs into its economy, we might expect that nationalized or otherwise socialized property would be the macro-level partner of WSDEs at the micro level. On the other hand, because traditional socialists have learned critical lessons about nationalized property (perhaps concerning its contradictory relationship with political democracy), alternative partnerships might emerge. Property ownership could be partly centralized and partly decentralized at regional and local levels. Property ownership could be shared between state entities at various levels and the workers in each WSDE. There might also be room found for some private individual ownership, shares, and stock markets. On the other hand, workers might reject these forms of property because of their close associations with private capitalist economies.

Presumably, WSDEs would accumulate experiences with and therefore come to choose among the alternative possible property ownership arrangements. In the past, capitalist organizations of enterprises found ways to adopt, adapt to, and invent various combinations of individual, partnership, corporate, and state ownership of productive property. Advocates of the transition from capitalist (private or state) enterprises to WSDEs will likely disagree and debate the strengths and weaknesses of the alternative property ownership arrangements that could coexist with WSDEs. That debate began long before the capitalist system achieved hegemony, continued during it, and will continue afterward. It has provoked an accumulated literature that should inform this debate and can be interrogated and rethought for the conditions and purposes of a new economic system in which WSDEs prevail over other organizations of work.

8.3 WSDEs and Markets

A parallel sort of reasoning applies to that other pillar of traditional socialism, the notion that state planning should displace markets as the mechanism of distributing productive resources and outputs. In that sort of socialism, broadened to include WSDEs as the prevalent organization of enterprises, government planning would distribute productive resources to and direct the inter-industry flows of outputs among WSDEs. Government plans would also govern the distribution of goods and services to consumers. Market exchanges would be marginalized or eliminated in such combinations of traditional socialism and WSDEs.

However, this is not the only way to link WSDEs to one another and to consumers. Markets offer another way. I do not wish to rehearse the thousands of years of literature evaluating the social costs and benefits of markets—or the last century's intense debates pitting proponents of capitalist markets against advocates of socialist planning. The point here is to stress the difference between the micro-organization of the enterprise and the distributional linkages among enterprises and between them and final consumers. WSDEs can coexist with planning or markets or combinations of both. From Yugoslavia to Mondragón and beyond, there are historical examples we can learn from.

The interactions of WSDEs with planning bodies will differ from their interactions with markets. The evolution of WSDEs will depend in part on whether they coexist with planning, markets, or combinations of them. The larger point here is that the internal organization of enterprises is different from the nexus of relationships among them and between them and consumers.

A basic component argument of the neoclassical economics that prevails in the world today asserts—and even claims to "prove"— that markets are "more efficient" than any government intervention, especially planning, could ever be. Not surprisingly, in state capitalist societies this argument provoked the converse counterargument, with proofs for the greater efficiency of socialist planning (sometimes phrased as greater "rationality"). As I argued earlier, the efficiency argument hangs on identifying and measuring all costs and benefits of either distributional mechanism. Yet that is not—and never has been—feasible. The costs and benefits of either run into an unknowable future. The project of identifying all potential consequences and measuring them in some common unit is simply impossible.

It follows, then, that efficiency claims and calculations, let alone "proofs" for them, cannot logically serve to evaluate markets versus planning or private versus socialized productive property—or indeed anything at all. How WSDEs will come to coexist with private versus socialized productive property and to coexist with markets versus planning will not be determined by spurious claims about their comparative efficiencies. It will be determined through the construction of particular, specific postcapitalist economic systems as they emerge in transitions from both private and state capitalist systems.

9 Economic and Political Democracy

To this point, I have been discussing WSDEs primarily in terms of democratizing the workplace, changing operations inside the enterprise, and, especially, reorganizing its production, appropriation, and distribution of surplus. In this chapter, I will turn to the important role of surrounding communities at various levels, from local to national and even international.

The reproduction of WSDEs is fostered, facilitated, and broadly supported by their members' similarly active democratic participation as residents in the governance of their local and regional communities. By definition a WSDE requires all workers to participate fully in directing their enterprises; this will be far easier to achieve and reproduce inside enterprises if those same workers are accustomed to functioning similarly in directing the communities where they reside.

145

Likewise, political democracy in the larger community, if it is to be more than merely formal, requires the economic democracy embodied in WSDEs. This argument is both theoretical and historical. Nothing will more effectively inspire and activate workers to become informed, competent, and full participants in the democratic governance of the communities in which they reside than functioning in that way inside their workplaces. However, modern capitalism precludes workers from democratic participation inside their enterprises. Thus, contemporary residentially based democracy (with elections based on where voters live, not work) rarely succeeds in drawing the mass of people into active, ongoing democratic political decision-making. Even when workers are not directly or formally excluded from real participation in governing their communities, their exclusion from directing activities where they work tends to build in them expectations of parallel exclusion where they live. Under such conditions, many (often most) workers lose interest in the political process and governance in general. Then they rarely participate beyond sometimes responding to candidates who seem to represent "at least some change" or "a lesser evil" or "passionate advocates" for some specific issue (e.g., gun control, abortion, gay marriage, immigration).

Habits of participatory behavior, assumptions about what is appropriate and "normal," expectations, and tastes for participatory power are developed in workplaces and carry over into residential communities, and vice versa. Participatory democracy at each social site depends on and fosters participatory democracy at the other. WSDEs need participatory democracy in the surrounding localities, regions, and nation for their own survival and will therefore encourage them.

9.1 Democracy in the Workplace

WSDEs also stimulate political democracy in another way: by developing an ideological argument out of their own need to survive. WSDEs, especially in their early stages of formation and growth, may encounter suspicion from people and enterprises used to the capitalist organization of production. WSDEs may be attacked for being utopian, inefficient, and so on. Against a host of such dismissive arguments, proponents of WSDEs have already and will increasingly deploy an argument about democracy. That argument begins by celebrating democracy as a basic social value, one at least verbally endorsed in modern societies by nearly everyone. In contrast, however, the democracy actually experienced in residence-based electoral systems gives people extremely limited control of what governments actually do. Beyond residential communities, in another and at least equally important part of social life—workplaces—democracy of any kind is disallowed. The majority of able-bodied adult citizens in most countries now spend most of their waking lives laboring in and preparing for workplaces. If democracy is a genuine foundational social value, it ought to govern the workplace first and foremost.

Yet workers in most modern capitalist corporations are required by law and/or custom to accept working conditions over which they exercise no democratic control. If they refuse, they can be fired—and the primary option available to them is to work for another employer under similarly undemocratic conditions. For most workers in capitalist systems, there is no democracy in the workplaces where they must spend most of their lives.

It is vital, then, to connect the transition from capitalist enterprises to WSDEs with the extension of political to economic democracy. Establishing and spreading WSDEs becomes part of completing modern society's limited democratization. Retaining the hierarchical capitalist organization of enterprises is, in fact, the obstruction of democratization. This line of argument also affirms that the extension of political to economic democracy accomplishes a crucial strengthening of political democracy as well. Workers who are required to learn the skills of participating fully in directing their WSDEs will be much more inclined to demand equal participation in their community-based politics. Likewise, workers from WSDEs will be far better prepared for such participation. In short, transition to WSDEs will strengthen political democracy.

Beyond extending political to economic democracy and thereby strengthening them both via mutual reinforcement, the specifics of such an extension merit consideration. The decisions of communities at the local and regional levels affect enterprises in countless ways. For example, curricula in schools affect labor productivity; public environmental protection programs affect enterprises by influencing illness and absence problems for employees; road building and maintenance affect traffic issues for enterprises; laws and judicial decisions influence disputes among enterprises and their adjudication; and publicly funded and directed research creates new products and new technologies that affect what enterprises produce and how they do so. In capitalist societies, enterprises have long understood and responded to the influence over their affairs exercised by political authorities. This is why corporations have devoted growing portions of their appropriated surpluses to lobbying and funding parties, candidates, and various kinds of political action committees.

9.2 Containing Democracy

Capitalist surpluses distributed to government in the form of taxes have largely aimed to reproduce capitalism generally. The additional capitalist surpluses distributed in the forms of lobbying expenses and political contributions have aimed to support specific capitalist industries and enterprises. Distributed capitalist surpluses in both forms have aimed at blunting systemic political risks in state as well as private capitalisms. In private capitalist systems, the boards and major shareholders of capitalist enterprises and those they make rich have long understood that even a limited democratic politics based on universal suffrage poses a systemic risk. The employees of capitalist enterprises—who compose, with their families, the vast majority—could find in their numerical voting strength the means to improve their economic position. They could, in short, utilize democratic politics to reduce and offset what they have lost because of an undemocratic economics. They could demand government intervention in the economy to their advantage and at the expense of capitalist enterprises' boards of directors, major shareholders, and the top 10 percent of income recipients and wealth owners. Workers, united for political effect, could vote for taxes and regulations to further these ends. They might push for workers' political ascendance, as the majority, to control the state and then, via the state, to control and even take over ownership of capitalist enterprises. That was, after all, a major thrust of traditional socialism over the last century. It represented one realization of the systemic risk politics represented to private capitalists and their wealthy dependents.

In the state capitalist systems that composed most actually existing socialisms, similar systemic political risks existed. The workers in state capitalist enterprises were, again, the majority. If united and focused, they could have used their numerical political strength to alter the economic decisions about what and how to produce and how to distribute the surpluses and to what social ends. They could have challenged the power and privilege of the managers and political officials who benefited by controlling their surplus.

Both private and state capitalisms have had to "manage" the systemic risk posed by the potential for workers to use politics to limit, offset, or end their losses from undemocratic workplace organizations. Private and state capitalisms expend portions of their appropriated surpluses to control and blunt that risk. Like spending portions of the surplus to provide security from criminals and outmaneuver competing businesses, spending to control the political landscape is another cost of capitalist business.

Where private capitalist enterprise prevails, dominant coalitions of parties (or factions within parties) funded by private capitalists can be assembled. Capitalists have to devote portions of their surplus to sustaining allied political, economic, and cultural organizations as the social base for such party coalitions. This especially includes the cultural organizations that originate and/or disseminate theories, religions, and other ways of understanding how the world works that serve their interests. To control politics requires shaping how the mass of people understand the workings of the world, what the Marxian theorist Antonio Gramsci analyzed as building a "hegemonic bloc." Where state capitalism prevailed, there was often only one major party. Then the hegemonic bloc had to be defined and organized by state capitalists from among groups or factions within that party. The basic processes were the same, but they had to be adjusted for the specifics of state rather than private capitalism.

The crucial point is that the capitalist organization of enterprises, both private and state, generates similar contradictions, tensions, and crises. The mass of workers, excluded from directing the capitalist enterprises in which they labor, can reasonably look to residence-based politics to counteract that exclusion and its effects. Universal suffrage and representative political democracy have sometimes opened up such possibilities within private capitalist systems. Socialist tradition and ideology could sometimes do likewise inside state capitalist systems. However, capitalists in both systems have also noticed those possibilities, seen them as threats, and found effective ways to limit and control them. They have built hegemonic blocs inside and outside of government to secure the reproduction of the social order they preferred. They have kept the workers from democratizing their enterprises—turning them into WSDEs. That in turn has kept the workers and their interests from directing the decisions on what, how, and where the enterprise produced or how to distribute the surplus it yielded. Capitalists' successes also reinforce the basic contradictions at the heart of the capitalist organization of production.

The workers in both kinds of capitalism sense their exclusion, politically as well as economically, from making the key decisions in what are endlessly hailed as "democratic societies" in one and "people's democracies" in the other. This sense leads to resignation, deepening cynicism, and hostility among many workers. Such feelings express themselves in massive disinterest in politics and in economics—beyond securing the weekly paycheck. Endless exhortations about the need to be involved and concerned and to participate in civic affairs—made by the duly appointed official exhorters in schools, churches, and political leaderships—become raw material for comics. Reactionaries transform those empty exhortations into imaginary "good old days" that would return if only their political projects were achieved.

9.3 Democracy and Crises

The historical irony is that the exclusion of the mass of workers from economic and political directorships also ends up costing private and state capitalism massively. Both variants of capitalism worked their way into major crises in part because of that exclusion; both had serious problems emerging from those crises for the same reason. For example, during the Great Depression, the combination of basically conservative Republican and Democratic political leadership allowed the 1929 crash to descend, by 1933, into 25 percent unemployment, mass impoverishment, and impending economic collapse. However, the mass of workers were then, exceptionally, able to break out of their resignation, cynicism, and despair. Under the leadership of the Congress of Industrial Organizations (CIO) and socialist and communist parties, they channeled their energies into a unified, focused, and mobilized counterhegemonic push. Roosevelt had drastically to change course. He was pressured from below to approve massive expenditures to benefit the bottom of the economic pyramid. This version of "trickle-up" economic policy, paid for in significant part by taxes on corporations and the rich, worked far better to moderate the crisis than the prior trickle-down policy had done. Private capitalist hegemony had weakened enough to enable a serious counterhegemonic thrust to get far enough to force a basic change in economic policy, if not to challenge capitalism as such.

To take another example, consider the second major capitalist collapse in the last seventy-five years, the one that began in 2007. For three decades before that crisis began, private capitalist hegemony was strong enough to roll back much of the social democratic welfare state regime installed by Roosevelt. That hegemony radically altered the distribution of wealth and income, returning the country to pre-1929 extremes of inequality. The predictable atrophy of consumer demand when real wages stopped rising in the 1970s was postponed by a debt explosion that hit its limits in 2007. (Flat real wages can only service rising household debts for so long.) In short, the economic effects of private capitalist hegemony contributed to a crisis of capitalism. Likewise, the political effects of that hegemony steadily destroyed the labor movement, as well as the communist and socialist parties that combined to produce the counterhegemonic thrust that turned Roosevelt around. So in recent years, despite a deep and lasting capitalist crisis, we remain tethered to a trickle-down economic policy.

Finally, to take an example from state capitalism, consider the economic crises that erupted in the 1980s in many actually existing socialisms. Those crises mobilized a mass of workers who had accumulated unaddressed grievances against the state capitalists. Partly because of their systematic exclusion from directing roles in the economy or in politics, their resentment could be mobilized in support of a return to private capitalism. In a sense, it was the reverse of a mistake made by so many in the CIO and in socialist and communist parties in the 1930s who saw a shift to state-managed capitalism as the solution to the problems of private capitalism.

The outcome of the crises in state capitalism might have turned out far differently if workers there had understood their system as a state form of capitalism. Such an understanding might have rallied massive support for a very different response to the state capitalist crises of the 1980s. That response would have argued that what failed in actually existing socialisms was neither state ownership of means of production nor state planning. What failed was the basic organization of production. Actually existing socialism failed to transform the internal capitalist organization of its enterprises into WSDEs. Thus, when crisis hit, angry and disaffected workers were resentful and uncooperative with the top-down measures imposed on them to cope with the crisis. Those workers could not overcome decades of exclusion and organize to support an alternative strategy for overcoming crisis. They could not see their way to advocate a policy for state capitalist crisis that stressed transition to WSDEs.

Working-class forces in private capitalist countries had been unable to respond to their grave crises by advocating transition to WSDEs in the 1930s. Working-class forces in state capitalist countries proved similarly unable to push for such a transition in the 1980s. It is time for those forces to put forward this micro-level demand and add the transition to WSDEs to their agendas for social change.

10 WSDEs in Modern Societies

Whether WSDEs are created as new enterprises or as products of transitions from differently organized enterprises—or, more likely, both—they will enter into complex relationships with the larger societies in which they develop. As enterprises, they will necessarily interact with other enterprises, both other WSDEs and enterprises organized differently (capitalist or otherwise). They will need to deal with government at all levels. They will likewise interact with consumers and, more broadly, politics and culture. In this chapter, I will focus on elaborating these relationships further and will offer a specific program for sharply expanding the scope and social presence of WSDEs.

WSDEs will interact with other enterprises in multiple ways. First, the physical inputs of WSDEs may need to be obtained from other WSDEs or from non-WSDEs. Likewise, the outputs of

WSDEs may well become physical inputs for other enterprises, both WSDEs and others. In short, every society in which WSDEs emerge will need to organize its inter-enterprise flows among and between WSDEs and differently organized enterprises. Market exchanges negotiated by the enterprises would be one way to organize such flows, government planning would be another, and all manner of combinations of market and planning would provide a large menu of distributional mechanisms.

10.1 The Competitive Success of WSDEs

Before exploring these relationships, it may be useful to consider claims that competition between capitalist and noncapitalist enterprises (including WSDEs) necessarily must lead and always has led to the same result: dominance of the former and disappearance of the latter. Such notions of some inherent unidirectional nature of economic development are common. Thus, for example, monopolies are said to destroy competition and big business to make small business disappear. However, neither theory nor historical evidence supports these notions.

Monopolistic enterprises around the world spend billions annually to secure their monopolies precisely because most understand their fragility. Monopolies can be and often are lost and replaced by competition in their respective industries. In fact, monopoly and oligopoly give way to competition as much as the reverse: for examples, consider the modern history of the US automobile, telephone, computer, household appliances, and other industries. The same applies to shifts between large and small business organizations. Just as small retail stores disappeared in the wake of chain stores and megastores like Walmart for middle- and lower-income people, something like the opposite happened for upper-income groups (who rejected shopping in them) and for the poorest (who could not afford shopping even in them). The latter two groups shopped more and more in small retail outlets: boutiques for the upper-income group and "convenience stores" for the poorest. In many countries, medium and small businesses succeeded in securing subsidies, tax exemptions, and other government supports equal or greater than those secured by big businesses. They thereby reversed or arrested transitions from smaller to larger business units.

If WSDEs organized mutual support and sufficient political strength, they too might prevail in competition with capitalist enterprises. The same result might follow if workers in WSDEs prove to be more productive than capitalist employees. If WSDEs sharply reduce the remuneration of managers, eliminate dividends, and use those funds instead for technological innovation, they might thereby outcompete capitalist enterprises unwilling or unable to do likewise. Successfully differentiating their products as being associated with democratic, noncapitalist work organization might help WSDEs to gain a competitive advantage over capitalist enterprises relying on conventional advertising.

Throughout the history of capitalism, when some communities established noncapitalist enterprises, these have sometimes shown themselves quite capable of successfully competing with capitalist enterprises. The best example today is the Mondragón Corporation in Spain, with more than eighty-five thousand worker-members and a fifty-year history of growth (www.mondragon-corporation.com). Of course, sometimes the competition between capitalist and noncapitalist yields the latter's defeat. The point is that no intrinsic or necessary outcome of that competition is discernible or logical. The complex of economic, political, cultural, and natural conditions will combine to determine both the emergence of WSDEs in modern capitalist societies and the outcomes of competition between them and capitalist enterprises. Among those conditions are the contending ways in which citizens in those societies understand WSDEs and their relationship to capitalism.

Depicting WSDEs as somehow intrinsically unsuccessful competitors of capitalist enterprises serves to exclude WSDEs from public consideration as alternatives to capitalism. It shuts off comparisons of WSDEs' strengths and weaknesses with those of capitalist enterprises. This effort to ban debate over alternative enterprise organizations in economics has historical parallels in politics. For example, monarchists sometimes insisted that representative democratic government was unviable and impossible: it would necessarily dissolve into anarchy, requiring reversion back to monarchy. There was thus no point in debating the strengths and weaknesses of monarchy versus democracy. Similarly, those who today fear debate over WDSEs versus capitalist enterprises seek to prevent it by inventing an inherent nonviability of WSDEs.

10.2 When WSDEs and Capitalist Enterprises Coexist

The emergence of WSDEs into contemporary societies would have all sorts of implications for differently organized enterprises. Workers in capitalist enterprises where they are excluded from directing—where they are exploited—will react in a variety of ways to the presence and growth of WSDEs in their communities. Technological innovations acceptable to capitalist enterprises may not be to WSDEs. WSDEs will attend to the quality of working conditions differently from capitalist enterprises. In short, the entrance of WSDEs into a society's mix of enterprises will change all of its economic processes and conflicts and thus its evolution. The specifics of such changes will vary with the quantity of WSDEs, their locations (in which industries and regions), and how they interact with the rest of society.

WSDEs and capitalist enterprises will, for example, manage their challenges and disappointments differently. Consider a WSDE troubled by the problem of falling revenues (because of lack of demand, technological backwardness, or shortage of inputs). That WSDE could well decide to lower individual wages and salaries and thereby enlarge the surplus available to solve the problem (via advertising, installing advanced equipment, securing new input sources, and so on). The workers who collectively lowered their individual wages would be the same workers who received and used the enlarged surplus to solve the problem. In contrast, workers in a capitalist enterprise would more likely resist such a solution since other people—the capitalists who exploit them—would receive and decide what to do with any extra surplus realized by lowering individual wages. Distrust accumulated from conflicts and struggles between capitalists and workers would contribute to such a result. Thus, WSDEs and capitalist enterprises would likely find and implement different responses to similar enterprise problems. Societies with different mixes of WSDE and non-WSDE enterprises would thus evolve differently.

One particular issue that often arises about WSDEs can be briefly addressed at this point. Could WSDEs ever attain the large size that has been reached by many modern multiproduct and multinational capitalist corporations (both private and state)? And if so, should they? There is, in principle, no reason why WSDEs could not attain comparable size. The issue they would then face replicates the problem of political democracy with large populations. A local vote for mayor is different from a national vote for president, yet it has proved possible for representative political democracy to accommodate size. A commitment to economic democracy will comparably find innovative ways to achieve democratic decision-making in larger bodies.

WSDEs are most easily understood as relatively small enterprises (fewer than a thousand workers) where the workers functioning collectively as their own board of directors can personally know one another, gather in subgroups and plenaries, and reach reasoned consensus on directorial decisions. Yet if a WSDE is successful in its production, finds a large demand for its products, and can integrate new workers smoothly and equally into its collective directorship apparatus, it may grow large. It will then face the same basic sort of issue faced by communities that grow or amalgamate into larger ones and yet wish to retain their representative democracy. The large WSDE may find that its ways of coping with its large size introduce all sorts of problems, limits, and compromises into its workers' collective directorship. It may then face (and variously resolve) internal tensions over the relative advantages and disadvantages of large size.

Yet WSDEs can opt against large size. They can choose to limit their sizes to hold onto a preferred version of workers' self-direction. Indeed, we might expect an ongoing tension within and among WSDEs in an economy because of differences among workers over the question of optimal enterprise size. Some WSDEs might reflect movements toward amalgamation, while others dissolve into smaller enterprises. Much the same happens among nations. Switzerland has resisted the movement toward European unification. Czechoslovakia split into two nations, while Germany unified its two parts. Various European nations are more or less enthusiastic to merge into one Europe. Similarly contradictory movements exist on the other continents as well. Tensions and shifts between larger and smaller WSDEs will characterize large and small capitalist enterprises and large and small units in a global system of nation-states.

Different sizes among WSDEs will result from many forces. However, one key force will be workers' evaluations of differences between larger and smaller enterprises. In WSDEs, workers will decide how to resolve the benefits and costs of size. In contrast, in capitalist enterprises, workers have little or no influence over this decision. In general, that disparity of influence has fueled the tendency towards mega-corporate capitalism, typically at workers' expense. The growth of WSDEs would change that.

10.3 WSDEs and the State: Economic Flows

Like their capitalist counterparts, WSDEs would find in the state a provider of services needed for successful enterprise performance, a taxing power, and a regulator. Both kinds of enterprises would be concerned with increasing the quantity and improving the quality of state services useful for their activities. Both would be concerned with maintaining or lowering the taxes charged to them. Both kinds of enterprise would be interested in adding, shaping, or removing state regulations according to their impacts on the achievement of their respective goals.

Sometimes, capitalist enterprises and WSDEs might find common ground—for example, in supporting the state's building and maintenance of transport facilities and other infrastructure, state-funded research, public education, and so on. However, WSDEs and capitalist enterprises will often make contradictory demands on the state. Struggles over state policies may become flashpoints of social tension between the alternative ways to organize production.

WSDEs will be concerned, as capitalist enterprises are, with what is taught in the public schools. In this case, the two kinds of enterprises will pursue sharply different goals. WSDEs will need schools to teach the benefits and modalities of collective behavior to prepare future workers for their positions in WSDEs. They will want schools to develop the aptitudes and teach the skills of a worker who is also an enterprise director. Thus the curricula should stress how to recognize and diagnose the problems of the enterprise as a whole, to draw upon alternative analytical disciplines and theories to fashion solutions, to design short- and long-run plans for enterprise change and growth, to divide tasks into subtasks and coordinate those responsible for the subtasks, and so on. In short, WSDEs need public schools to teach all students how to design and direct large group activities and how to give and receive orders within a community of equals.

These have never been the goals of most public schools in economies where capitalist enterprises prevail. Instead, private and public schools for the rich provide education designed especially for directors, upper managers, and their professional staffs and allies. The bulk of public schools provide the basics needed by the mass of workers—reading, writing, and arithmetic—as well as social conditioning to follow orders from their directors and managers in capitalist enterprises.

In the widest sense, WSDEs and capitalist enterprises will find themselves in competition that goes beyond economics (capturing market share, higher profits, faster growth rates) to draw in political and cultural institutions such as the state. The competing demands on public education, for example, will lead both sides to seek public support and political allies. Each side will pressure the state to respond to its agenda for state policies, state expenditures, taxes, and regulations. The coexistence of WSDEs and otherwise organized enterprises will pressure each to outperform the other. Each will seek state assistance in this quest. Each will be threatened by the successes of the other. The ideological celebration of competition typical in societies with chiefly capitalist enterprises may well become muted when that competition is broadened to include WSDEs.

WSDEs will differ from capitalist enterprises in the decisions they reach regarding the location of production. WSDEs will be less likely to solve the problems of their enterprises by relocating production to distant places. The directors of WSDEs are the same people as the workers who would either lose their jobs by relocation or suffer its material and psychic costs. Plant closings, outsourcing, job exports, and so on would occur in extreme cases, and then only if accompanied by state support for all the adjustments involved. Capitalist corporations might enjoy a competitive advantage over WSDEs due to their far greater flexibility about relocating production to take advantage of cheaper wages, lax environmental controls, and other profit opportunities. This would likely provoke intense struggles between capitalist enterprises, WSDEs, and their supporters over how to assess the larger social costs and benefits of relocating production versus finding other avenues to solve enterprise problems.

To take one historical example: for many years, capitalists competed by hiring low-paid child labor and using air- and water-polluting technologies. Eventually, mass oppositions made these strategies harder to pursue or, in some cases, illegal. Capitalists had then to find other ways to solve their competitive problems. They complained bitterly that important means of competitive growth had been blocked. But eventually they either complied or else relocated to avoid compliance. Many of those capitalists who stayed and complied found other competitive strategies, some of which proved more advantageous than child labor or toxic technologies ever had.

The arrival of WSDEs would change the classic struggle over enterprise relocation between labor, unions, and left parties on the one hand, and on the other, capitalists demanding maximum freedom from state interference with their relocation decisions. With WSDEs, there will be ongoing demonstrations of the viability and, in some cases, superiority of solving enterprise problems in ways other than relocation. The survival of WSDEs over time, especially in industries and regions that capitalist enterprises have abandoned, would undermine capitalists' arguments for their freedom to relocate.

Finally, we may anticipate the possible objection that WSDEs' commitments to retain and build on local production facilities and systems would "deprive" less developed nations of the industrial jobs that might otherwise have gone there. Capitalists who arrive after having secured all sorts of costly local benefits from cash-strapped local governments thereby reveal themselves. They never lose their interest in new relocation possibilities. The historical record is filled with examples of the positive benefits of arriving capitalist enterprises being offset by the negative consequences of their subsequent relocation a few years later.

Rather than exporting the footloose capitalist enterprise model (alongside such capitalist enterprises themselves), all nations would be better served if we exported the WSDE model instead. Less developed countries, even more than the developed ones, need secure, stable jobs in enterprises that do not maneuver to get exemptions from regulations concerning wages, working conditions, and the environment. If a genuine commitment exists to assisting economic development in the places that need it most, the WSDE model would be far preferable to facilitating capitalist competition and its "race to the bottom" among all economies.

10.4 WSDEs and the State: Political Flows

Earlier in this book (in section 7.1), I distinguished one kind of worker inside an enterprise, whose labor produces a surplus, from another kind whose labor enables the production of surpluses. I illustrated the distinction by comparing the software workers who produce new games with the cleaners who tidy up the workspace each evening. Producers and enablers: the two kinds of workers, I argued, have some common features and some distinctions. They are all employees of an enterprise, but they relate differently to the reproduction of the enterprise. The first group produces the outputs that contain the surplus (the excess of the value added by those laborers over the value paid to them as wages and salaries). The second group, the enablers, provides crucial conditions for the surplus-producers to work. They keep records, provide security, maintain clean conditions, provide legal counsel, and perform countless other tasks just as important for the reproduction of the enterprise as the production of its outputs.

On the basis of the commonalities and the differences between these two basic kinds of enterprise employees, I developed a corresponding specification of their respective participations in a WSDE. In a sense, this is a description of the political relationship between the two kinds of workers within WSDEs. In contrast, private and state capitalisms have tended to obliterate the distinction. All workers are treated as undifferentiated "wage-earners" or "proletarians" or "employees." When, sometimes, a difference is recognized, it is relegating to a secondary status analytically—for example, such distinctions as "white collar" versus "blue collar" or "mental" versus "manual" laborers. In my analysis, however, the difference between the two kinds of workers is crucial, especially for analyzing their political relationships inside WSDEs and the political relationships between WSDEs and their surrounding communities.

For an enterprise to be a WSDE, two defining conditions must be satisfied. First, there can be no exploitation—no appropriation and distribution of a surplus by anyone other than its direct producers. The collective surplus-producers are likewise the collective appropriators and distributors. Second, there must be democratic direction of the enterprise by both kinds of its workers. Thus both surplus-producing and surplus-enabling workers must together—by collaborating democratically—make certain key directing decisions. They must decide how big a surplus will be produced and how much surplus labor will be performed by the surplus-producing workers. They must also decide which outputs will be produced, how that will be done technologically, and where it will be done geographically. Finally, they must also decide how the appropriated surplus will be distributed by the producers/appropriators: in what portions, to whom, and for what purposes.

To satisfy these conditions, a WSDE needs a board of directors that includes the two different kinds of workers: the surplus-producers and the enablers. Such a board would allocate the task of appropriating and distributing the surplus to its subgroup of exclusively surplus-producing workers. That secures the absence of any exploitation within the WSDE. The entire board—both surplus-producers and enablers—would collaboratively and democratically make all the other directorial decisions. That secures democratic worker self-direction.*

Now I need to extend and expand this discussion of the democratic collaboration between the two kinds of workers inside WSDEs to direct the enterprise. My goal is to specify an equally democratic relationship between both kinds of workers within a

---

* This division within the WSDE parallels a typical division within capitalist boards of directors. In the latter, individuals who are simultaneously top managers (such as CEOs) and members of a corporation's board of directors are excluded from

WSDE and its surrounding communities (local, regional, and national). One basis for this specification is that those communities must live with the results of the decisions and activities of the WSDE. The other basis is that WSDEs are affected by the conditions and activities of their surrounding communities and the directing decisions made by their governing representative democratic bodies. The democratic values that animate the concept of and social movement for WSDEs require that the communities and the WSDEs become democratically interdependent.

The governing principle should be that residents and workers participate in each other's decisions to the extent that each is affected by the other's decisions. If residents are organized in a representative democracy, their representatives should participate in directing the WSDEs with which they are interdependent. Likewise, all the workers within a WSDE should themselves—or via representatives— participate in the decisions taken by residence-based governing bodies. The particular modalities of this democratic codetermination between enterprises and residential communities will, of course, be worked out, challenged, and adjusted in ways the people involved will develop. There will be tensions, debates, and struggles over those modalities, just as there have been over every other political system. However, these will reflect the specific conditions of WSDEs and democratically governed residential communities.

In societies where WSDEs are the prevailing organization of production, capitalists will no longer occupy a crucial political position.

---

one key board function: they cannot serve on the compensation committee that negotiates top managers' pay. The goal is to lessen problematic conflicts of interest internal to the corporation. WSDEs exclude surplus enablers from the one board activity of appropriating and distributing the surplus. The goal is to avoid a conflict of interest—any exploitative relationship—internal to them.

Capitalists' use of the surpluses they appropriate will no longer dominate politics. We will no longer have capitalists making political use of the resources typically at their disposal—the surpluses they appropriate. Instead, the community of workers who direct WSDEs will be the prevailing political partner of residence-based governing bodies. Two different but overlapping communities—one work-based in the WSDE and one residence-based—could then tie together economic and political democracy. They might finally realize democracy, which under capitalism was never allowed to go beyond very limited electoral formalism.

11 Program and Personnel for Increasing WSDEs

There are many ways to increase the presence and effects of WSDEs in modern societies. In this chapter, I introduce a few of them, chiefly to demonstrate their availability, practicality, and cost-effectiveness. Most of these are ways to move forward in the United States by responding to today's political opportunities. Of course, those opportunities vary from place to place within the United States and beyond. They are always changing. The following discussion will thus remain at a fairly general level.

11.1 A Federal Jobs Program

The capitalist crisis that descended on the world late in 2007 has left a long legacy of unemployment. In the United States, unemployment has roughly doubled and has so far resisted all efforts to return it to pre-crisis levels. Moreover, those levels were already staggeringly wasteful. Millions of unemployed workers coexist with more than 20 percent unutilized productive capacity (as reported by the Federal Reserve). Enormous potential output was thereby lost in and by a capitalist system that needed it to address pressing social problems. Millions of homes have been foreclosed upon, educations interrupted, and relationships and health damaged by continuing high unemployment and underemployment.

When the US economy suffered its last major capitalist meltdown, President Roosevelt undertook a direct federal jobs program to reduce massive unemployment. Since 2007, the alternative program preferred by both the Bush and Obama administrations—government incentives for private capitalists to hire workers—have clearly failed to solve the problem. Another federal jobs program could make a major difference in overcoming or at least reducing the dysfunction of a capitalist system that cannot provide jobs for people who want and need to work. Moreover, a federal jobs program could also provide new freedoms of choice and opportunity to workers by including WSDEs.

Unlike Roosevelt's approach in the 1930s, a jobs program today should include provisions to provide founding capital to workers willing to commit to building WSDEs. Learning from and adapting the example of Italy's very successful 1985 Marcora Law, which enabled workers to take over enterprises that were in crisis, the US government could offer unemployed workers here a similar choice. Instead of a period of receiving regular unemployment payments, they could choose to get the total of such payments in advance as initial capital for a WSDE. The condition would be that they find a group of other unemployed people willing to make the same choice and pool the funds for the WSDE.

Many advantages could flow from such a program. It would use government funds not merely to sustain the unemployed but rather to assist their immediate, self-motivated transition back into productive employment. It is therefore less a program costing new government funds than one redirecting existing funds to better outcomes. We could expect greater commitment to the success of such a WSDE by the workers involved, given that its failure would not trigger unemployment benefits for the workers involved and that its potential benefits would go far beyond wages. In addition, such an experimental program could provide people with concrete, immediately observable examples of WSDEs. They could examine and consider a different organization of production—a personal work environment very different from the traditional, hierarchical capitalist enterprise. For the first time in US history, workers would begin to acquire some freedom of choice between alternative work experiences. For that freedom of choice to become real for most people, WSDEs would have to proliferate quickly from their beginning in this proposed federal jobs program.

No doubt, new WSDEs enabled by some adaptation of a Marcora-style law would require all sorts of government support. These might include, for example, technical assistance, subsidized or guaranteed credit access, temporary tax exemptions, preferential purchasing of WSDE goods and services by government agencies, and so on. The rationale for providing such potential supports for WSDEs is much like the rationale for actual supports provided now to small businesses, minority-owned businesses, and businesses in less developed countries targeted for assistance: it is in our collective interest to do so. In this case, the interest lies in moving toward genuine freedom of choice among alternative organizations of production: working within democratically organized WSDEs versus within capitalist enterprises.

Choice between different workplace experiences is not the only new freedom we can anticipate. With the spread of WSDEs, consumers would also acquire new freedoms of choice. For example, if markets were to be the means of distribution among enterprises and consumers, the coexistence of capitalist enterprises and WSDEs would allow consumers to choose between their respective outputs. Much as US consumers can now at least sometimes select products that are "organic," "fair trade," or made in alternative countries, they could—when WSDEs became common—select products made in alternatively organized enterprises. If governments required product labels to reflect the organization of their production, consumers' purchases of WSDE versus capitalist commodities would be votes for WSDE and against capitalist enterprises.

Finally, consider the mutual gains from a possible alliance between supporters of WSDEs and supporters of a "green" New Deal. They might press jointly for a federal jobs program addressing both their goals. Both of them could likewise join those concerned with other specific outputs a federal jobs program might target (for example, child and elder care, cultural enrichment of the sort achieved by the Works Progress Administration in the 1930s, and so on). The political force of such an alliance might approach that of the alliance among the CIO and socialist and communist parties in the 1930s, which won the most massive federal jobs program in US history, filling more than twelve million jobs between 1934 and 1941.

11.2 Alliances with Cooperative Movements

There is a long history in the United States and in many other countries of cooperative enterprises—including worker or producer co-ops. In many cases, associations have been created and sustained over many years that serve various needs of these cooperatives.

A movement for WSDEs should seek alliances with the existing co-operative movement. Immediate campaigns for laws facilitating the growth and viability of existing cooperatives might be the basis for obtaining, in return, the support of existing cooperatives for the formation of new WSDEs. For example, there might be a joint campaign for a US version of the Marcora Law and a change in the tax code to ease the tax burdens on existing cooperatives. Business and other schools need to be encouraged to teach courses on co-ops as a form of business students can learn about and aspire to.

Finally, WSDE supporters should consider a common electoral effort. It would include, on one side, existing co-op organizations, their customers, and their sympathizers. On the other would be those newly drawn to WSDEs as a central part of the solution to capitalism's crises and long-term dysfunction. Combining forces, they might well frame a program and campaign to elect candidates favorable to building up a large and growing cooperative sector of the economy.

11.3 Alliance with the Trade Union Movement

Unions struggling with capitalist employers need additional weapons to reverse their long decline in numbers and social influence. A new relationship with existing producer cooperatives and the social movement for WSDEs could help turn the tide. Strikes, boycotts, and other actions against capitalist employers could be strengthened if there were institutions and mechanisms to provide the workers involved in such actions with a credible new strategic option. Suppose that workers could actually stop working for an unsatisfactory capitalist employer and easily work instead in a cooperative setting. Suppose that long before grievances with particular capitalists grew into such actions, labor unions began working with existing co-op institutions and the social movement for WSDEs to prepare them to better compete with capitalist enterprises. Suppose that small, modest producer co-ops were established. Capitalist enterprises would have to worry about such noncapitalist competitors not only in terms of the price and quality of their competing outputs and their potential growth. They would have a new concern: competition with an enterprise that offers an alternative internal organization, a different work experience, and a different vision and path to a new economic system.

Under these conditions, when capitalists provoke, threaten, or impose strikes, lockouts, plant closings, or relocations, they will face a new response. Instead of anxious workers and unions deciding between caving in or calling the capitalist's possible bluff, their alliance with co-ops and a movement for WSDEs gives those workers and their union a new weapon in their struggle. They are ready to take over and operate the plant or enterprise. They have assembled the expertise, built up their members' awareness and excitement about such an endeavor, cultivated connections with other co-ops locally, nationally, and internationally, and perhaps even built up capital reserves or credit to counter-threaten capitalists in a new and potentially economy-changing way.

Co-ops, labor unions daily battling capitalist employers, and the fast-multiplying critics of capitalism revealed and inspired by the Occupy Wall Street movement could fashion a new version of the past alliances of unionists and progressives. This time the alliance could coalesce around concrete alternative workers' institutions—WSDEs—developing alongside unions' struggles with capitalist employers. The October 2009 announcement of an agreement between the United Steelworkers Union and the Mondragón federation of producer cooperatives in Spain represents an initial, important interest in some of these possibilities. Many more alliances along such lines should be explored.

11.4
The "Organic Intellectuals" of the WSDE Movement

The Occupy Wall Street movement mobilized a sizable number of younger workers. They have been shocked, depressed, and angered by the results that contemporary capitalism has been delivering to them for decades. They had anticipated and schooled themselves to qualify for jobs, incomes, and lifestyles that are no longer available and are not about to return anytime soon.

The revenge of the right wing was to mobilize its constituents to reject, and if possible erase, what it demonized as the "liberalism" of the 1960s and remnants of the New Deal. The right promised that prosperity would follow the political ascendancy of neoliberal economics (including deregulation of the market, privatization, and further decimation of unions and the left). It promised a return to an idealized "good old days" based on reversion to a social conservatism built on religious fundamentalism. Capitalism's latest phase of globalization-cum-monopolization-cum-financialization since the 1970s needed to control the state in its service and therefore required a mass political base. The Republican Party gathered the usual white, conservative, rural, suburban, small business, and variously nativist groups to secure that base. But most of its constituent parts were shrinking in size and commitment to the party. Only the socially conservative religious fundamentalists were growing and seemed willing to provide militants in support of the Republicans.

At the same time, stagnant real wages after the 1970s, the lengthening work hours of ever more family members, rising personal debts, and shrinking unions contributed to draw the mass working-class base of the Democratic Party away from political activism and engagement. The party became more dependent on financial support from big business and proved unable or unwilling to prevent rightward political shifts in government policies. From a high point of intense activity in the 1960s, broadly left and center-left movements—those advocating at least some basic changes in the US distribution of wealth and power—went into a deep decline, their leaders and militants often drifting into inactivity or depression.* The collapse of actually existing socialisms around the world in the late 1980s and after reinforced the decline. There seemed no alternative to a resurgent private capitalism trumpeting its inevitability even more loudly and self-confidently than communist leaders in Eastern Europe had declared theirs a few years earlier.

However dispirited it became, the left and center-left in the United States—and elsewhere—never disappeared. Leftists watched after the 1970s as virtually every critical prediction of capitalism's destructive tendencies was realized. These included concentration of capital into ever-larger units, rampant financialization, and imperialism (rechristened as "globalization" to mask the steady relocation of manufacturing and then service-sector jobs out of the United States), as well as wars, speculative bubbles, and massive capitalist crises. Anger and frustration accumulated on the left. With the stunningly rapid national and even international spread of the Occupy Wall Street movement in late 2011, an explicit protest movement began to crystallize.

---

* What did not stop were the often intense but more narrowly defined and focused single-issue movements, such as those against racism, sexism, and homophobia and for immigrants' rights and environmentalism.

The Occupy movement broke through decades of left resignation about the possibility and potential mass support for challenging the resurgence of private capitalism. The Occupy critique focused on capitalism's unacceptable concentration of wealth and power. It explicitly welcomed and articulated direct challenges to capitalism. It reopened communication with the declining labor movement in the interests of active collaboration and mutual reinforcement. It reopened connections with and reactivated interest in what needed to be learned from older anticapitalist movements.

Occupy reopened an explicit debate about the social costs of capitalism. In the United States and beyond, the capitalist emperor's latest outfit stands revealed. The systemic question "What is to be done?" is on the agenda again. Occupy opened the space for and the urgency of that question in millions of minds. And if the experiences of the first wave of socialism in the twentieth century are not the models for today, then what about them is worth preserving, rejecting, or redesigning today? What new contributions to conceiving a postcapitalist alternative can help focus and build upon what Occupy Wall Street began?

Part of the answer to these crucial questions is the concept of and movement for WSDEs, which can speak to those active in or inspired by Occupy struggles precisely because WSDEs emerge from but also go well beyond traditional socialism. WSDEs represent a basic critique of capitalism—both private and state—and also a concrete alternative to them. However, the analyses that show and elaborate these points need to be developed and disseminated. A new WSDE-based social alternative needs its "organic intellectuals"—to borrow a powerful idea from Antonio Gramsci—if it is to be realized.

By organic intellectuals, I mean, in part, those excited by WSDEs as possible centerpieces of a new social movement for modern societies.

I also mean individuals inclined and skilled enough to find effective means to communicate their excitement and thereby build such a movement. The left has always existed in tension between two basic dimensions. On the one hand, the left needs and desires to be concrete and practical, to have its feet on the ground, with direct responses to people's immediate needs and solutions for today's problems. On the other hand, it needs to have and project its utopian dimensions. Those include its visions for what could solve not only today's problems, but rather the underlying structural conditions that keep regenerating them. Utopian dimensions also include a clear vision of an alternative set of structural conditions that people believe might work and are therefore worth fighting for as an alternative to a deteriorating status quo.

Capitalism has generated its own organic intellectuals. In the United States and elsewhere, academic departments of economics have worked to train them at both undergraduate and graduate levels. Undergraduate courses focus chiefly on capitalism's extraordinary excellence in allocating scarce resources among competing demands and generating income distributions that justly reward all contributors to production. Graduate economics programs elevate such utopian claims into formalized models that claim to show how and why capitalism yields a general optimally efficient equilibrium that maximizes the welfare of all market participants.*

The organic intellectuals of the WSDE movement can present both practical possibilities (as in section 10.1 above) and utopian visions

---

* Precisely because academic economics departments emphasize utopian claims about capitalism's tendency to optimize efficiency and economic justice, courses in its practical dimensions have been relegated to a different academic location: business schools. For a discussion of the currently contesting paradigms of economic theory and analysis championed by hegemonic and counterhegemonic economists, see Wolff and Resnick, *Contending Economic Theories.*

of a socialism that is far more democratic than the standard examples from the twentieth century. By doing so, they may be able to persuade the Occupy movement and the millions it has engaged that WSDEs belong on the agenda for social change. The program for increased WSDEs needs to support and build—in universities, labor unions, social movements, and beyond—the meetings, discussions, courses, and centers that can generate and train organic intellectuals.

11.5 A New Independent Political Party

As WSDEs grow and proliferate, they will acquire and develop organic intellectuals who produce and elaborate their criticisms of capitalism and their programs for social alternatives. Given contemporary capitalism's difficulties, support will likely broaden and deepen a struggle for basic social change that includes WSDEs as a major component. The conditions will thus emerge for a political party to advocate such change and contest for the governmental power to accomplish it.

No existing major party shows the slightest inclination to go in such a direction. Small left parties may do so, singly or in groups. Or perhaps a new independent party will need to be developed. In either case, modern electoral arenas, notwithstanding their structural obstacles to basic social change, are simply another place where social criticism and advocacy for WSDEs should be articulated. Political parties can achieve legislative gains for the social expansion of WSDEs. Elections and representative legislatures are not the only, or necessarily the central, locations for struggles over social change, but leaving them to the enemies of the movement for WSDEs is tactically unnecessary and strategically unwise.

Conclusion

The word "cure" in this book's subtitle deserves a qualifying comment. It does not mean some state of completion, some end to problems, contradictions, and further change. On the contrary, it means moving from one set of problems that have become increasingly unbearable to a new and different set that we prefer. WSDEs—and an economic system founded on them—will no doubt have contradictions and tensions. The people caught up in them will struggle over them, much as people have struggled in and over capitalism's contradictions. However, the struggles over WSDEs will differ from those over capitalist (or other exploitative) organizations of production because they will no longer involve the tensions and conflicts between those people who produce and those who appropriate the surpluses. Similarly, because a system of WSDEs will likely have much less inequality of income among participants in the work of enterprises, that inequality too will figure far less prominently in its struggles.

To consider a historical parallel, the cure of emancipation for slavery did not mean that ex-slaves put economic or other problems behind them. They no longer struggled over the problems associated with being the property of other persons; instead they engaged with new problems. In the United States, that meant entering into a capitalist system and confronting new forms of racist violence and economic exploitation and exclusion. Struggles in and over capitalism replaced the old struggles in and over slavery. Yet a clear global consensus counts the transition from slave to capitalist systems as a major monument to progress, one that should be extended and made irreversible.

Recognizing the limits and contradictions of transitions from one economic or social system to another can usefully accompany passionate commitment to such transitions. Those who earlier saw the needs and reasons to move beyond private capitalism to various sorts of state capitalism included many who prematurely declared that the socialism of their dreams and the forms of state capitalism that actually emerged were the same. But there were always also those who saw the contradictions and limits of state capitalism and questioned their equation with socialism.

The histories of private and state capitalism over the last century and the accumulated dilemmas of both now offer us strong reasons and evidence to believe that we must and we can do better. Examining the limits of both kinds of capitalism returns us to their shared commitment to an internal organization of production based on exploitation, inequality, and hierarchy. That organization's persistence played a major role in preventing state capitalism from evolving into the genuine alternative to capitalism so many hoped for—and paved the way for reversion to the less-regulated neoliberal capitalism that now provokes intense social conflicts across the globe.

The transition of enterprises from their capitalist internal organizations to the genuine alternative of WSDEs emerges as a new program out of the history of capitalisms over the last century. The elaboration and clarification of WSDEs in theory are one part of a way forward now. Another part is the concrete practical establishment and expansion of WSDEs. Together, the theory and practice of WSDEs compose a powerful and attractive program that belongs on serious agendas for social change today.

Index

Numbers

Also from Haymarket Books

Detroit: I Do Mind Dying: A Study in Urban Revolution
by Dan Georgakas and Marvin Surkin
Detroit: I Do Mind Dying tracks the extraordinary development of the Dodge
Revolutionary Union Movement and the League of Revolutionary Black
Workers as they became two of the landmark political organizations of the
1960s and 1970s.

Essays, by Wallace Shawn
"Full of what you might call conversation starters: tricky propositions about
morality . . . politics, privilege, runaway nationalist fantasies, collective guilt,
and art as a force for change (or not). . . . It's a treat to hear him speak his
curious mind." —O Magazine

Howard Zinn Speaks: Collected Speeches 1963 to 2009,
by Howard Zinn, edited by Anthony Arnove
"Howard Zinn—there was no one like him. And to hear him speak was like
listening to music that you loved—lyrical, uplifting, honest." —Michael Moore

*Ours to Master and to Own: Workers' Control from the Commune
to the Present*, by Immanuel Ness and Dario Azzellini
"Ness and Azzellini have made a major contribution in producing this in-
sightful and exciting collection of essays on the question of workers'
control . . . it is timely and offers great strategic insight." —Bill Fletcher Jr.

On History: Tariq Ali and Oliver Stone in Conversation
Their dialogue brings to light a number of forgotten—or deliberately
buried—episodes of American history, from the dynamic radicalism of the
Industrial Workers of the World to the ongoing interference of the United
States in Pakistani political affairs.

The Paris Commune: A Revolution in Democracy,
by Donny Gluckstein
By paying particular attention to the historic problems of the Commune
and critical debates over its implications, Gluckstein reveals its enduring
lessons and inspiration for today's struggles.

About Haymarket Books

Haymarket Books is a nonprofit, progressive book distributor and publisher, a project of the Center for Economic Research and Social Change. We believe that activists need to take ideas, history, and politics into the many struggles for social justice today. Learning the lessons of past victories, as well as defeats, can arm a new generation of fighters for a better world. As Karl Marx said, "The philosophers have merely interpreted the world; the point, however, is to change it."

We take inspiration and courage from our namesakes, the Haymarket Martyrs, who gave their lives fighting for a better world. Their 1886 struggle for the eight-hour day, which gave us May Day, the international workers' holiday, reminds workers around the world that ordinary people can organize and struggle for their own liberation. These struggles continue today across the globe—struggles against oppression, exploitation, hunger, and poverty.

It was August Spies, one of the Martyrs targeted for being an immigrant and an anarchist, who predicted the battles being fought to this day. "If you think that by hanging us you can stamp out the labor movement," Spies told the judge, "then hang us. Here you will tread upon a spark, but here, and there, and behind you, and in front of you, and everywhere, the flames will blaze up. It is a subterranean fire. You cannot put it out. The ground is on fire upon which you stand."

We could not succeed in our publishing efforts without the generous financial support of our readers. Many people contribute to our project through the Haymarket Sustainers program, where donors receive free books in return for their monetary support. If you would like to be a part of this program, please contact us at info@haymarketbooks.org.

Shop our full catalog online at www.haymarketbooks.org or call 773-583-7884.

About the Author

© Don Usner

Richard D. Wolff is Professor of Economics Emeritus, University of Massachusetts, Amherst. He is currently a Visiting Professor in the Graduate Program in International Affairs of the New School University in New York. Wolff has also taught economics at Yale University, City University of New York, University of Paris I (Sorbonne), and the Brecht Forum in New York City. In 2010, Wolff published *Capitalism Hits the Fan: The Global Economic Meltdown and What to Do About It,* also released as a DVD. He is the author, most recently, of *Occupy the Economy: Challenging Capitalism,* with David Barsamian (San Francisco: City Lights Books), and *Contending Economic Theories: Neoclassical, Keynesian, and Marxian,* with Stephen Resnick (Cambridge, MA, and London: MIT University Press). Wolff hosts the weekly hour-long radio program *Economic Update* on WBAI, 99.5 FM, New York City (Pacifica Radio). He writes regularly for *The Guardian,* Truthout.org, and *MRZine.* He has been interviewed on *Democracy Now!, Charlie Rose,* Al Jazeera English, Russia Today, National Public Radio, *Alternative Radio,* and many other radio and TV programs in the United States and abroad. The *New York Times Magazine* named him "America's most prominent Marxist economist." His work can be accessed at rdwolff.com. Wolff lives in Manhattan with his wife and frequent collaborator, Dr. Harriet Fraad, a practicing psychotherapist (see podcasts on psychology and economics at www.rdwolff.com).